Evaluator's Handbook

Lynn Lyons Morris
Carol Taylor Fitz-Gibbon

Center for the Study of Evaluation
University of California, Los Angeles

SAGE PUBLICATIONS Beverly Hills/London

The *Program Evaluation Kit* was developed at the Center for the Study of Evaluation, University of California, Los Angeles. Copyright of this edition is claimed until December 31, 1988. Thereafter all portions of this work covered by this copyright will be in the public domain.

The *Program Evaluation Kit* was developed under a contract with a National Institute of Education, Department of Health, Education and Welfare. However, the opinions expressed herein do not necessarily reflect the position or policy of that agency, and no official endorsement should be inferred.

The *Program Evaluation Kit* is published and distributed by Sage Publications, Inc., Beverly Hills, California under an exclusive agreement with The Regents of the University of California.

For information address:

Sage Publications, Inc.
275 South Beverly Drive
Beverly Hills, California 90212

Sage Publications Ltd
28 Banner Street
London EC1Y 8QE

Printed in the United States of America

International Standard Book Number 0-8039-1071-1
Library of Congress Catalog Card No. 78-58658

NINTH PRINTING, 1982

Table of Contents

Editor's Acknowledgements

At the end of a long bout of work such as preparation of the *Program Evaluation Kit,* people get sentimental. I can see why—after such a long haul, this is the only bit of emotion one can muster. The last appropriate action here is to briefly, but with deep gratitude, acknowledge the contributions of the people without whom the *Kit* could not have been produced in this form.

Foremost recognition is due to Carol Fitz-Gibbon, my collaborator on the books of the *Kit.* Carol's good mind and accurate sense of how best to say things helped set the tone and flavor of the books. Her experience as a junior high school teacher kept us mindful of people in the schools—those doing and administering education whom we felt would comprise a good part of our audience. Carol is a master at explaining difficult concepts in a concrete way so that issues can be understood by even the least technically oriented.

Thanks are also due the reviewers who examined and commented on parts of either the field test draft of the Kit or the current books. Among these were James Burry, Leigh Burstein, Ernest House, Ward Keesling, Edward Kifer, Leonard Klibanoff, Alex Law, Gaea Linehart, Fred Niedermeyer, Rodney Skager, Robert Stake, Rand Wilcox and Jennie Yeh. We owe particular thanks to Jason Millman, formative evaluator *par excellence,* who reviewed several manuscripts in minute detail. One of these, with annotations, was returned to us with a lengthy discussion of a technical point scribbled on the back of one page. The last sentence of this discussion read, "Please excuse my handwriting, but I'm writing this on the bus."

The small staff assembled at the Center for the Study of Evaluation to accomplish the job of producing this Kit in camera-ready form couldn't have been more dedicated or good natured. Each member became an accomplished and expert contributor to the whole operation. The heart of the production effort was, from my perspective, Donna Anderson Cuvelier who kept track of manuscript preparation—typing, proofing, and dealing with the typesetter and layout artist. In addition to this, she typed most of the final manuscript and formatted the worksheets in *How To Calculate Statistics* and the Step-by-Step Guides of the *Evaluator's Handbook.* She was assisted in all of this by Ruth Paysen, Able Typist, and expert decoder of bad handwriting.

Another indispensible member of the staff was Michael Bastone, technical editor, whose grasp of major issues in educational research helped keep most of the procedures recommended in the Kit technically honest. Marlene Henerson and James Burry, both excellent manuscript editors, kept us from too badly abusing English grammar.

The work of Lou Orsan, graphic designer, can be seen on every one of the Kit's 1100-odd pages. Lou worked long hours, past the financial limits of the contracted job and with a loyalty that one seldom receives from a commercial contractor to a project.

Two people on the staffs of CSE and Sage Publications fueled the perpetual motion machine that was necessary to keep this large, lumbering project from dallying. On the Sage side, Sara McCune threatened, cajoled and pushed. From the CSE side, Adrianne Bank pleaded, begged and pulled.

Finally, I want to express loving gratitude to Ivan Mendelsohn because of whom—and at times in spite of whom—I found the strength to bring such a large project to completion.

Lynn Lyons Morris

Los Angeles, California
August 1978

Chapter 1

An Introduction to the Program Evaluation Kit

The *Program Evaluation Kit* is a set of books intended to assist people who are conducting evaluations of educational programs. The scope of its potential use is broad. Because it comprises a set of step-by-step *procedural guides,* the Kit can advise a person conducting elaborate evaluations of far-reaching and many-faceted programs; or it can help people as they gather, analyze, and interpret information for almost any purpose—whether it be surveying peoples' attitudes, observing a program in action, or measuring student achievement.

In addition to suggesting step-by-step procedures, the Kit introduces and explains concepts and vocabulary common to evaluation. You can therefore use it for training or staff development. The Kit is intended to be useful to people with extensive experience in evaluation as well as those who are encountering program evaluation for the first time.

Components of the Kit

The *Program Evaluation Kit* consists of the following eight books:

1. This book, *The Evaluator's Handbook,* is meant to help you get started, to serve as an organizer for the evaluation, and to provide a directory to the rest of the Kit. The introduction contained in Chapter 1 calls attention to the critical issues surrounding program evaluation. Chapter 2, entitled *How to Play the Role of Formative Evaluator,* describes the diversified job of a person who enters into a helping relationship with a program's staff. Chapters 3, 4, and 5 contain step-by-step guides for organizing and accomplishing three types of evaluations:

- A formative evaluation calling for a close working relationship with the staff during program installation and development (Chapter 3)
- A standard summative evaluation based on measurement of achievement, attitudes, and/or program implementation (Chapter 4)
- A small experiment, a procedure most likely to be of interest to a researcher or to the evaluator who wishes to either conduct pilot tests or evaluate a program aimed toward a few measurable objectives (Chapter 5)

The *Handbook* concludes with a Master Index to topics discussed throughout the Kit.

2. *How To Deal With Goals and Objectives* provides advice about using goals and objectives as methods for gathering opinions about what a program should accomplish. The book then describes how to organize the evaluation around them. It suggests ways to find or write goals and objectives, reconcile objectives with standardized tests, and assign priorities to objectives.

3. *How To Design a Program Evaluation* discusses the logic underlying the use of research designs—including the ubiquitous pretest-posttest design—and supplies step-by-step procedures for setting up experimental, quasi-experimental, and time series designs to underpin the collection of evaluation data. Six designs, including some unorthodox ones, are discussed in detail. The book outlines the use of each design, from initial choice of program participants to analysis and presentation of results. Finally, it includes instructions about how to construct random samples.

4. *How To Measure Program Implementation* presents step-by-step methods for designing and using measurement instruments—examination of program records, observations, and self-reports—to accurately describe how a program looks in operation. The first chapter discusses *why* measuring implementation is important and suggests several points of view from which you might describe implementation, for instance, scrutinizing the consistency of the program with what was planned or writing a naturalistic description free of such preconditions. Its second chapter is an outline of the implementation section of an evaluation report.

5. *How To Measure Attitudes* should help the evaluator select or design credible instruments for attitude measurement. The book discusses problems involved in measuring attitudes—including peoples' sensitivity about this kind of measurement and the difficulty of establishing the reliability and validity of individual measures. It lists myriad sources of available attitude instruments and gives step-by-step instructions for developing questionnaires, interviews, attitude rating scales, sociometric instruments, and observation schedules. Finally, it suggests how to analyze and report results from attitude measures.

6. *How To Measure Achievement* focuses primarily on the tests administered for program evaluation. The book can

be used in several ways. In case you plan to purchase a test, it helps you find a published test to fit your evaluation. To this effect, the book lists anthologies and evaluations of existing norm- and criterion-referenced tests and supplies a Table for Program-Test Comparison. The step-by-step procedure for completing this table directs you to compute numerical indices of the match between a particular test and the objectives of a program. If you want to construct your own achievement test, the book presents an annotated guide to the vast literature on test construction. Chapter 4 lists, as well, test item banks and test development and scoring services. The final chapter describes how to analyze and present achievement data to answer commonly-asked evaluation questions.

7. *How To Calculate Statistics* is divided into three sections, each dealing with an important function that statistics serves in evaluation: summarizing scores through measures of central tendency and variability, testing for the significance of differences found among performances of groups, and correlation. Detailed worksheets, ordinary language explanations, and practical examples accompany each step-by-step statistical procedure.

8. *How To Present an Evaluation Report* is designed to help you convey to various audiences the information that has been collected during the course of the evaluation. It contains an outline of a standard evaluation report; directions and hints for formal and informal, written and oral, reporting; and model tables and graphs, collected from the Kit's design and measurement books, for displaying and explaining data.

The step-by-step procedures that comprise the bulk of most of the books have been written with the understanding that the exact form of an evaluation activity varies with the situation. Where the evaluator's role—formative or summative—affects what the evaluator does, suggestions about alternative courses of action are provided.

Kit Vocabulary

A few basic concepts are used over and over throughout the *Program Evaluation Kit*—the term *program* for example.

A *program,* as referred to in the Kit, is anything you try because you think it will have an effect. This is a purposely broad definition. A program is anything you do that can be described so that you can do it again, if you want to. A program might be a tangible *thing,* such as a set of curriculum materials; or a *procedure,* like the use of volunteer aides; or an *arrangement* of roles or responsibilities, such as a reshuffling of the administrative office of a school district. A program might be a new kind of scheduling, like a longer lunch hour; or it might be a series of *activities* designed to improve students' attitudes toward school. A program is anything definable and repeatable. In evaluation, *program* is synonymous with *project* or *innovation.*

When you *evaluate* a program, you *collect information* about what the program looks like in operation and about the effects it is having. Sometimes this information is used

to make decisions about the program, for example, how to improve it, whether to expand it, or whether to discontinue it. Sometimes evaluation information is ignored or has only an indirect influence on decisions about the program. *How* the information will eventually be used does not define evaluation, however. Program evaluation is the collection of information about a program in a manner that is credible enough to make it *potentially* useful. The focus of this Kit is the collection, analysis, and reporting of credible information.

Credibility means believability. The word occurs many places in the Kit because the criterion of credibility separates "good" evaluation information from "bad." The job of the evaluator is to describe a program and its outcomes to various groups who need this information. The likelihood that the results of an evaluation will be heard, discussed, and used is increased if these results are seen to be accurate. *Notice that credibility is relative to the opinions of people who receive your report.* A community of scientists will make different demands for proof than will a group of parents—and the scientists will not always be the more demanding group! Recognition that information has to match the audience is critical if you are to adapt to the political context of an evaluation—and nearly all evaluations have such a context.

Generally an evaluation has a *sponsor.* This is the person or organization who requests the evaluation and usually pays for it. If the members of the school board request an evaluation, they are the sponsors. If a federal agency requires an evaluation, the agency is the sponsor.

Evaluations always have an *audience.* An evaluation's findings are of course reported to sponsors, but there might be other recipients of the information as well. A common audience for formative information collected during program development consists of the people running the program—the *program's staff, planners, and managers.* Another audience might be students, parents, special interest groups, or the local community. If the program will be exported to additional sites, or written about in widely circulated publications, then the broader scientific or educational community comprises one evaluation audience. Audiences, in short, are the groups that you will have in mind as you conduct the evaluation. If your audiences share a common point-of-view about the program or are likely to find the same evaluation information credible, consider yourself fortunate. This is not always the case.

For some evaluations, of course, the roles of evaluator, sponsor, and audience are all played by the same people. If teachers decide to evaluate their own program, then they will be at once the sponsors, the audience, the program managers, *and* the evaluators. Though the Kit treats these roles as distinct, it is recognized that people sometimes fill overlapping functions.

A decision made by the evaluator that affects the credibility of the evaluation for many audiences is selection of a *design.* An *evaluation design* is a plan determining *when* evaluation instruments or measures—tests, questionnaires, observations, record inspections, interviews, etc.—will be administered and *to whom.* Design provides a basis for comparing the results of measurements to a standard. This

TABLE 1
Some Models of Program Evaluation

Model	Emphasis	Selected References
Goal-Oriented Evaluation	Evaluation should assess student progress and the effectiveness of educational innovations.	Bloom, B. S., Hastings, J. T., & Madaus, G. F. *Handbook on formative and summative evaluation of student learning.* New York: McGraw-Hill, 1971. Provus, M. *Discrepancy evaluation for educational program improvement and assessment.* Berkeley, CA: McCutchan, 1971.
Decision-Oriented Evaluation	Evaluation should facilitate intelligent judgments by decision-makers ·	Stufflebeam, D. L. (Ed.). *Educational evaluation and decision-making.* Itasca, IL: F. E. Peacock, 1971.
Transactional Evaluation	Evaluation should depict program processes and the value perspectives of key people.	Rippey, R. M. (Ed.). *Studies in transactional evaluation.* Berkeley, CA: McCutchan, 1973. Stake, R. E., et al. *Evaluating the arts in education: A responsive approach.* Columbus, OH: Charles E. Merrill, 1975.
Evaluation Research	Evaluation should focus on explaining educational effects and devising instructional strategies .	Campbell, D. Reforms as experiments. *American Psychologist,* 1969, *24,* 409-429. Cooley, W. W., & Lohnes, P. R. *Evaluation research in education.* New York: Irvington Publishers, 1976.
Goal-Free Evaluation	Evaluation should assess program effects based on criteria apart from the program's own conceptual framework.	Scriven, M. Prose and cons about goal-free evaluation. In W. J. Popham (Ed.), *Evaluation in education: Current applications.* Berkeley, CA: McCutchan 1974.
Adversary Evaluation	Evaluation should present the best case for each of two competing alternative interpretations of the program's value with both sides having access to the same information about the program.	Levine, M. Scientific method and the adversary model: Some preliminary suggestions. *Evaluation Comment,* 1973, *4*(2), 1-3. Owens, T. R. Educational evaluation by adversary proceedings. In E. R. House (Ed.), *School evaluation: The politics and process.* Berkeley, CA: McCutchan, 1973.

standard might be the performance of program participants prior to the program or the scores of a comparable group of non-participants. Comparison to a standard gives you some perspective on the magnitude of the effect the program has had and helps you decide whether it was indeed the program that brought about the outcomes you have measured.

The Evaluation Model On Which the Kit Is Based

As soon as you begin to read the literature in the field of evaluation, you will encounter *evaluation models*. Descriptions of some of the more prominent ones, with principal references, appear in Table 1.

These models serve mainly to conceptualize the field and draw the boundaries of the evaluator's role. In addition, they provide a vocabulary so that people describing evaluation issues can speak from a common basis. If you plan to spend considerable time working as an evaluator, the references in Table 1 should help you catch up on what evaluators have said about their craft. Additional readings of interest to evaluators are listed in the *For Further Reading* section at the end of the chapter.

This Kit has drawn at least some of its various prescriptions about how to evaluate a program from most of the models in Table 1. Each model is appropriate to a particular set of circumstances; and since the Kit's purpose is to help you to decide what to *do* when confronted with different situations, it is natural that its advice would sound at different times as though it emanated from different evaluation models.

The principal theoretical basis on which the *Program Evaluation Kit* rests is not represented in the table. The CSE Evaluation Model, because of its relative lack of prescriptiveness about how evaluations should be conducted, is difficult to pigeonhole.

The CSE Evaluation Model

Most of the evaluation models described in Table 1 outline *how* their various proponents believe evaluations should be conducted. The CSE model, shown in Figure 1, focuses by contrast primarily on *when* to evaluate. *It points out phases during the development of a program during which various audiences might effectively use credible information.*

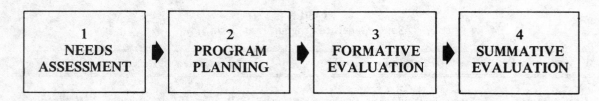

Figure 1. Stages of the CSE Evaluation Model

Though the CSE evaluation model might more appropriately be called a model of program development, it provides a useful picture of the exchange of information that can take place among evaluator, sponsor, staff, and community during the life of a program. It also shows ways in which the evaluator's role should alter to fit changes in the information needs of various audiences as the program matures.

The CSE program development model, at least in its major outlines, has guided evaluation theory, practice, and training conducted by the Center for the Study of Evaluation since the late 1960's. The purpose behind using such a model is to give people a common framework for thinking about and discussing things that might otherwise be too complicated to deal with clearly. For this reason, the model is highly idealized. Its fit to the *actual* realities of evaluating programs will be discussed as the chapter progresses.

The CSE model, shown in Figure 1, views program evaluation as the process of selecting, collecting, and interpreting information for the purpose of keeping various audiences informed about a program. Usually these audiences will use the information to make decisions. The kinds of decisions that need to be made about a school program depend on the *stage of development* of the program. The process of creating school programs can be seen as taking place in four phases.

Needs assessment

The first phase in the cycle of program development is *Needs Assessment* during which a program's *goals* are determined. In settings where the program is intended to respond to the wishes of community members, information gathering during the needs assessment can reach parents, teachers, students, school board members, and the broader community. Where a program addresses a single subject area, a needs assessor might only solicit the opinions of experts and curriculum specialists in that area. At times, the sponsor or funding agency more or less *declares* a need by making money available for programs aimed toward certain goals. Sometimes an effort is made to verify through testing or surveys that the needs perceived by the audience do in fact exist. It is to remedy most critical "needs," or to achieve high priority goals, that the program is then planned.

Every program goes through a needs assessment phase regardless of who sets the goals or how informally they are determined.

Program planning

The second phase in program development is *Program Planning.* Ideally, teachers, curriculum experts, and others will plan a program to meet the highest priority goals determined by the needs assessment. At times, the need to reach certain goals will prompt planners to design a prototype program from scratch, putting together materials, activities, and administrative arrangements that have not been tried before. Other situations will require that they purchase and install, or moderately adapt, an already existing program. *Both* situations qualify as program planning—something that had not occurred previously in the setting is installed for the purpose of meeting announced goals. Plans should be laid at this time for evaluation of the program, but they rarely are.

The first two phases of the evaluation model show its preoccupation with uncovering and delineating the program's own *goals.* A needs assessment sets goal priorities; program planning designs or purchases a program to reach them. Implicit in this is the model's one prescription about how evaluations should proceed: they should address, at least partly, the *goals* of the program's constituency and/or those the program planners and staff claim the program will accomplish. *The evaluator, whose job it is to provide information about its progress, then, should begin by looking at the program's goals.* Not all evaluation models make this prescription. Scriven, for one, suggests that evaluators work from a fixed set of humanitarian supraprogram goals, regardless of the program's unique objectives. Stake's "responsive" approach requires that the evaluator describe what the program looks like and seems to do regardless of its own *or* society's aims.

You will notice that throughout the Kit the advice is to "start by looking at the program's objectives." It seems that you will be most likely to find what your audience wants to know by looking first in the place toward which they are pointing! This, of course, does not mean that you cannot search for other program effects as well or spend time just describing what the program looks like. These are all important, and the Kit's various step-by-step guides and *How To* books point out unplanned effects and processes you might look for.

Formative evaluation

Phase three of the CSE Evaluation Model is *Formative Evaluation.* Formative evaluation requires collecting and sharing information for program improvement. While a program is being installed, the formative evaluator works to provide the program planners and staff with information to help adjust it to the setting and improve it.

Suppose, for example, that teachers have heard of a new chemistry program at a conference and want to try it out. Purchases are made and boxes are delivered. This will be the first year of the new program. What kind of decisions will have to be made? Eventually, of course, people will want to know how good the program is compared with other possible programs, and whether or not to continue with the program. However, these are questions that cannot be answered right away. They must await a *summative* evaluation that asks about the *overall value* of a program.

Before the program *as a whole* can be described, summarized, and perhaps judged, it must be allowed to get on its feet, and develop to the point at which it is functioning day-to-day as effectively as possible.

This developmental program phase—perhaps a few days or weeks, or maybe years, depending on the program—is the time for *formative* evaluation. Ideally, the program's sponsors should give a new program a chance to make mistakes, solve problems, and reach the point where it is running smoothly before they decide how good it is. All the time a program is in this developmental stage, full of trial and error, the staff is trying to implement it properly, revise the program to meet their particular situation, and make sure participants are making progress. If there is an evaluator at this stage of the program, she is charged with providing information that helps to improve the program.

The formative evaluator, therefore, *becomes involved* with the program. She works closely with program managers telling them how the program looks and what progress is being made, and helping them to develop the program to be as effective as possible in meetings its goals.

Early during program implementation, the exact nature of the program and the manner in which it is expected to achieve its goals should be made explicit. The formative evaluator, therefore, not only helps to develop the program, but also to conceptualize *what the program is* and *how it works*. Since this conceptualization is an essential precondition for summative evaluation, formative evaluation lays the groundwork for summative.

Summative evaluation

Summative evaluation, the fourth phase in program development, looks at the *total impact* of a program. It differs from formative evaluation in its timing and audience, and in the evaluator's relationship to the program. When a program has passed its developmental stage and is functioning as intended, it is ready to be summarily described and perhaps judged. This judgment is made by the people in a position to determine whether or not to continue the program, whether or not to expand the program, and whether or not to recommend the program for use in other schools or districts. These decision-makers may be principals, school board members, funding agencies, teachers, or parents.

Ideally, because the summative evaluator represents the interests of the sponsor and the broader community, he should try *not* to interfere with the program. The summative evaluator's function is *not* to work with the staff and suggest improvements while the program is running, but rather to collect data and write a summary report showing what the program looks like and what has been achieved. Ideally, the summative evaluator does not get involved with the program beyond making measurements. This detachment presumably is possible because such evaluation should examine only mature programs whose serious problems have already been worked out. If a summative evaluation is to be credible, the summative evaluator must be free to report negative findings.

Political realities, of course, tend to make such an idealized summative evaluation rare in practice. Discussions of the difficulty of producing objective summative evaluations point to three causes:

1. Regardless of who commissions the evaluation, directives to the evaluator usually require that he serve an ambiguous formative/summative function. Most evaluators are asked to work on improvement of the program *and* to write a summary report. The summative evaluator, therefore, scrutinizes a program in which he may have developed a personal stake, and objectivity is often lost.

2. Many funders request that the project staff hire its own summative evaluator. Because this evaluator is essentially in the employ of the local staff and may wish to receive commissions to evaluate in the future, he is loath to report negative findings. Evaluations conducted under these circumstances understandably err in the direction of over-praise. Some funding agencies even request that the program staff itself conduct the summative evaluation.

3. Few sponsors funding programs take the hard line, consumer advocacy point-of-view expressed in CSE's definition of summative evaluation. The prestige of a foundation or a department of the government, after all, comes from funding *effective* programs. Objectivity is often lost in summative evaluation because of fear of negative results. Negative results are seen as serving no one's benefit in the political arena where summative evaluators must live and work.

Unfortunately, this state of affairs keeps in operation programs of doubtful merit, preventing more effective ones from receiving funding. Most of the remedies suggested for the problem ask that summative evaluations be commissioned by agencies independent of the funders of the program. While these solutions are being worked out, however, you are likely to find yourself working as a summative evaluator in the exact political situation described here. You might, in other words, experience pressure to produce a favorable report. The best response to this is to follow your own conscience. Many evaluators deal with this problem by focusing on areas in which the program seems most likely to have good effects and then dispassionately reporting results in these areas. Evaluations of this sort are biased in terms of choice of *what* to study. However, clear and credible data collection can ensure an objective picture of the program from that point on. Reporting the results with a mention that the choice of what to depict was partly motivated by a desire to put the program in the best possible light violates no one's ethics.

To summarize, the CSE Evaluation Model outlines four stages of program development where information collection is helpful: needs assessment, program planning, formative evaluation, and summative evaluation. Since planners, sponsors, teachers, and community members could need information at any of these stages, evaluators might be needed to assist in any of these activities. Although this Kit is concerned primarily with formative and summative evaluation, many of its resources can assist in needs assessment. And to the extent that program planning requires collecting opinions, checking on student learning, or planning for the evaluation of the new program, the Kit will be useful during the program planning stage as well.

Conceptualizing Your Own Evaluation

"We'd better have an evaluation of Program X," someone could decide and then appoint you to carry out that decision. Proceed with this caution:

Your first act in response to this assignment should be to find out what evaluation means in this instance. Find out what is expected. What information will the evaluation be expected to provide? Does the sponsor or another audience want more information than you can possibly provide? Do they want definitive statements that you will not be able to make? Do they want you to take on an antagonistic or advocate role toward the program that you cannot in good conscience assume?

Failure to reach agreement about the exact nature of the evaluation to be conducted can lead to:

- Wasted money and effort—data are collected which are of no use to anyone
- Frustration—the evaluator feels she has wasted her time
- Acrimony—the sponsors feel they did not get what they asked for or expected

Step 1 in any evaluation condenses to one word: Negotiate!

As soon as you have accepted the assignment, assemble for yourself a clear picture of what you will be expected to do. This conceptualization will have four major components, each negotiated with your sponsor and audiences:

1. A decision about what these people really want when they say they want an evaluation
2. Selection of an evaluation design and measurement instruments based on what the audience will accept as credible information
3. Choice of a reporting style, that is, the extent to which you will report hard data as opposed to informal or qualitative information; and whether you will write technical reports, brief notes, or just confer with the staff

4. Delineation of what you can accomplish within the constraints of the evaluation's budget and political situation.

Determining What People Really Want When They Say They Want an Evaluation

The sponsor who commissions your evaluation might have in mind any one of *five* kinds of activities that could be called evaluation. Since each requires a different approach and various amounts of time and money, it is crucial that you clarify which definition prevails in your own situation. A request for an evaluation may turn out to be a charge to collect information:

- To conduct a needs assessment
- To describe what the program looks like in operation
- To measure whether goals have been achieved
- To help planners get and keep the program running smoothly—what the CSE Model calls formative evaluation
- To help the sponsor and others in authority decide the program's fate—summative evaluation

The boxes on pages 11 to 13 describe the five kinds of activities usually conducted under the title *evaluation*. Each is characterized by the question most likely to be in the sponsor's mind, some typical questions that might be generated around the main question, the activity that could occur, and finally the kinds of decisions that could result. Since the CSE Model's depiction of formative and summative evaluation encompasses the activities required for all the other kinds of evaluation described in the boxes, the *Program Evaluation Kit* contains enough information to help you perform any of them.

Evaluation Credibility

In addition to finding out what your audiences want to know, you will need to discover what they will accept as credible information. The credibility of your evaluation will, of course, be influenced by your own credentials. The audience will be less skeptical of your results if it thinks you know what you are doing. Their willingness to accept without question what you report will be based on other criteria as well. For one thing, they will take account of your allegiances. An evaluator must be perceived as free to find fault—whether or not she does. This means that you should not be constrained by friendship, professional relations, or the desire to receive future evaluation jobs. In addition, audiences will believe what the evaluator reports to the extent that they see her as representing themselves. The program staff, for instance, will be suspicious of a formative evaluator who will write a summary report at year's end to the funding agency. The agency, on the other hand, will read the report suspiciously if it suspects that the evaluator's formative work has put her on "their side." Because of these credibility problems, evaluators with ambiguous formative-summative job descriptions have to arrive at a determination of their *primary* audience through negotiation.

Questions on the minds of the sponsors and audiences

What needs attention?
What should our program(s) try to accomplish?
Where are we failing?

Appropriate labels for this kind of evaluation

Needs assessment
Organizational review

Kinds of questions the evaluator might pose

What are the goals of the organization or community?
How can goal priorities be determined?
Is there agreement on the goals from all groups?
To what extent are these goals being met?
What are the areas in which the organization is most seriously failing to achieve goals?
Where does it need to plan special programs or revise old programs?

Kit components of greatest relevance

How To Deal With Goals and Objectives
How To Measure Achievement
How To Measure Attitudes
How To Measure Program Implementation

Comment

Many requests for "evaluation" actually require a needs assessment. By probing, the evaluator might discover that the aim of the evaluation is neither to decide between continuing or dropping a program—summative evaluation—nor to develop detailed, specific activities to improve a program—formative evaluation. Rather, the sponsor wants to discover weaknesses or problem areas in the current situation which can eventually be remedied. Watch particularly for this substitution of "evaluation" for "needs assessment" when the program to be evaluated is large and complexly organized, with many goals, components, and staff roles: "Our nursing program needs evaluating" or "We need to evaluate our food services." Notice especially that a needs assessment frequently is used to make public implicit goals and/or to re-examine and critique existing goals.

Decisions and actions likely to follow a needs assessment

The decisions following a needs assessment usually involve allocation of money and effort to meet high priority needs. The activity that *should* follow is planning of programs—educational, organizational, whatever—addressed to the identified needs. Note that needs assessment differs from formative evaluation not only in the typical size or scope of the program under investigation, but more particularly in the fact that the formative evaluator *follows up* the identification of weaknesses. He works with the staff to attempt improvements *during the course* of the evaluation. In a needs assessment, on the other hand, the survey of needs is itself the end product.

Questions on the minds of the sponsors and audiences

What is happening in Program X?
What does it look like?
What do people experience?
How much does it vary from site to site?

Appropriate labels for this kind of evaluation

Description of program implementation
Program documentation
Evaluation of program processes

Kinds of questions the evaluator might pose

How many participants and staff are taking part?
When? How often? Where?
Is the program running on schedule?
Is the program being implemented according to plan?
Have the proper materials been purchased and are they being used?
What is a typical daily schedule?
How are time, money, and personnel allocated in the program?
What activities do participants in the program become involved in?

Kit component of greatest relevance

How To Measure Program Implementation

Comment

Description of program implementation focuses solely on the activities, materials, and administrative arrangements that comprise a program. It does not include a description of the *results* of program activities as would a formative or summative evaluation. The audience wants a description of who is doing what in Program X, or of how a requirement that such-and-such take place has been interpreted by program planners and developers across sites.

If this is your situation, be sure to ask if the audience or sponsor wants to compare programs or alternative versions of the same program over sites. In any case, be sure to *make it clear that you will not be relating program activities to outcomes.* For many audiences, a description of what is taking place is sufficient information for making decisions about the program. This is particularly true when the program is designed to reflect a philosophy or theory of how schools or organizations should be run in order to achieve long-term goals that cannot be immediately measured. In such a case, the evaluator's job is to collect evidence about the manner in which the theory or philosophy is being put into practice by program personnel.

Decisions and actions likely to follow program documentation

Sponsors and audiences are likely to judge the program on the basis of whether or not they think the activities occurring are valuable in themselves or will *probably* be effective in achieving other goals.

Questions on the minds of sponsors and audiences

Is Program X meeting its goals?

Appropriate labels for this kind of evaluation

Measurement of goal achievement
Objectives-based evaluation

Kinds of questions the evaluator might pose

What are the goals of the program?
How can they be measured?
What do measures show about the degree of goal attainment?

Kit components of greatest relevance

How To Deal With Goals and Objectives
How To Measure Achievement
How To Measure Attitudes

Comment

For this kind of limited evaluation, the evaluator promises only to measure the extent to which the program's highest priority goals are and are not being achieved. Some of these goals might be affective, such as satisfaction with the program; and others might be cognitive, such as arithmetic achievement. Program goals are usually stated in terms of student outcomes.

If your evaluation matches this situation, it is important to emphasize that you will not be able to state whether *the program alone* is responsible for the results you observe; and you will certainly be unable to say whether some other program would have been better. Simply looking at goal achievement, in other words, usually provides a poor basis for judging a program's *comparative* merits. If a statement about degree of goal achievement is all you will be able to produce, your results can still be of some use. Determining whether achievement measures up to set standards that have been carefully thought out does give a basis for at least tentative conclusions about the program's quality. And even though a reading program, for example, might not be the sole cause of the reading achievement of children in the program, it is the program that bears responsibility in the school setting.

**Decisions and actions likely to
follow measures of goal achievement**

Clarification and measurement of goals often helps planners and staff to better focus their activities on goals and make revisions in areas where goals are failing to be achieved. An evaluation that involves only measures of goal achievement will be cheaper than a full-scale formative evaluation where the evaluator helps the staff to choose among alternative program changes, and then in turn monitors the effectiveness of these.

Questions on the minds of sponsors and audiences

How can the program be improved?
How can it become more efficient or effective?

Appropriate label for this kind of evaluation

Formative evaluation

Kinds of questions the evaluator might pose

What are the program's goals and objectives?
What are the program's most important characteristics—materials, activities, administrative arrangements?
How are the program activities supposed to lead to attainment of the objectives?
Are the program's important characteristics being implemented?
Are they leading to achievement of the objectives?
What adjustments in the program might lead to the attainment of the objectives?
Which activities are best for each objective?
Are some better suited to certain participants?
What problems are there and how can they be solved?
What measures and designs could be recommended for use during a summative evaluation of the program?

Kit components of greatest relevance

All of them

Comment

Formative evaluation encompasses the thousand-and-one jobs connected with helping the staff to get the program running smoothly. It might even include conducting a needs assessment. Certainly it will involve some attention to monitoring program implementation and achievement of goals. In order to improve a program, it will be necessary to understand how well a program is moving toward its objectives so that changes can be made in the program's components. Formative evaluation is time-consuming because it requires becoming familiar with multiple aspects of a program and providing program personnel with information and insights to help them improve it. Before launching into formative evaluation, make sure that there actually is a chance of *making changes* for improvement—if no such possibility exists, formative evaluation is not called for.

**Decisions and actions likely to follow a
formative evaluation**

As a result of formative evaluation, revisions are made in the materials, activities, and organization of the program. These adjustments are made throughout the formative evaluation period.

Questions on the minds of sponsors and audiences

Is Program X worth continuing or expanding?
How effective is it?
What conclusions can be made about Program X or its various components?
What does Program X look like and accomplish?

Appropriate labels for this kind of evaluation

Summative evaluation
Outcome evaluation
Consumer testing
Evaluation research

Kinds of questions the evaluator might pose

What are the goals and objectives of Program X?
What are Program X's most important characteristics—materials, activities, administrative arrangements?
Why should these particular activities reach its goals?
Do the activities lead to goal achievement?
What programs are available as alternatives to Program X?
How effective is Program X in comparison with alternative programs?
How costly?

Kit components of greatest relevance

All of them

Comment

The goal of summative evaluation is to collect and present information needed for summary statements and judgments of the program and its value. If you are a summative evaluator, you should try to provide a *basis against which to compare the program's accomplishments.* It is a good idea to contrast the program's effects and costs with those produced by an alternative program that aims toward the same goals. This nearest competitor might be a previous program from which data are available. It is preferable, however, to examine a rival program in existence simultaneously. Of course, there will be situations where the program *cannot* be evaluated by contrasting its results with those produced by competitors. In these cases, participants' performance might be compared with a group receiving no such program at all or with that of similar groups of students in previous years. Your standard for comparison might have to come from the norms of the achievement test you administer or from a comparison of program results with the goals identified by the program designers or the community at large.

Be careful to notice instances where summative evaluation is inappropriate. An accurate summary statement cannot be written, for instance, about a program that is still developing. Unless, in fact, a program has clear and measurable goals, and consistent replicable materials, organization, and activities, the program is not suited for summative evaluation.

**Decisions and actions likely to
follow a summative evaluation**

Summative evaluations result in recommendations to continue or discontinue the program or to expand or cut it back.

Another determiner of how seriously the audience listens to your results is the *method* you use for gathering information. Methods of data gathering include the evaluation design; the instruments administered; the people selected for testing, questioning, or observation; and the times at which measurements are made. When you choose instruments and designs, or construct a sampling plan, remember this: *You cannot count on your audience to accept as credible the same sorts of evidence that you consider most acceptable.* People are usually skeptical, for instance, of arguments they do not understand. You might have noticed that when reports filled with complicated data analysis are presented, people stay quiet until a few experts have given their opinions. Then everyone discusses the opinions of the experts.

Unless your audience expects complex analyses, you should keep your data gathering and analyses straightforward. Think of yourself as a *surrogate*, delegated to gather and digest information that your audience would gather on its own, were it able. Keep a few representative members of the evaluation audience in mind, and ask yourself periodically: "Will Mr. Carson see the value in doing this analysis?" A good way to find out, of course, is to ask Mr. Carson.

Remember, as well, that the general public tends to place more faith in opinions and anecdotes than do researchers—at least usually. If you plan to collect a large amount of hard data, you will have to educate people about what it means.

Reporting Style, Budget, and Other Constraints

Reporting style refers to the relative weight your report gives to presenting quantitative data as opposed to less formal qualitative narratives. If sponsors or audiences want to receive from you a rich description of what happens in a program, full of anecdotes so that readers feel that they have "been there," then this is what you will report. A different style of evaluation might emphasize objective measurement. If sponsors and audiences want to see "hard data"—tables, figures showing results of questionnaires, observations, structured interviews, measures of achievement, etc.—then you need to know this from the start.

What your reports contain and how they are delivered will mutually affect one another. Credibility requirements and reporting style should therefore be negotiated early. It could turn out that the data the audience wants, or the kind of reports it requires, do not suit your own talents or biases.

Regardless of what information is desired or how it will be reported, the breadth and depth of the evaluation will be determined by the amount of time the evaluator can devote, by constraints on who, where, and when he can measure, and by limitations on what he can ask. Time available for the evaluation is mainly determined by the budget. Constraints on data collection come from the political surround. Find out which sites, people, and topics are off limits for you.

Some Important Concerns You Might Have About Program Evaluation

The decision to assume an evaluator's role toward a program of any sort raises many questions and issues—some practical, some philosophical. The remainder of this chapter introduces four of them:

1. What good can come from an evaluation?
2. What about all the charges that evaluation results are seldom, if ever, used?
3. Why use control groups and evaluation designs?
4. How does an evaluator decide what to measure?

What Good Can Come From an Evaluation?

Consider the current situation. Throughout education, hundreds of innovative ideas are being tried in classrooms, schools, and districts:

- *One of the teachers in our school visited England, and now four teachers are trying to duplicate British Infant School classrooms.*

- *In our district we have decided that reading is the single most important skill, and we have launched an all-out campaign to get the scores up.*

- *The state is funding junior high math resource centers. They cost quite a lot of money, and we are wondering if they are worth it.*

- *The ninth grade general math teacher is motivating the low achievers by having them regularly tutor fourth graders. It is a lot of trouble, but it seems to work really well.*

- *Our district has ESEA Title I funds. We have fully individualized the primary grades in our five elementary schools.*

- *The 12th graders in Mrs. James' Contemporary Problems Class are getting Friday afternoons off to go on field trips of their own choosing.*

To the above mentioned examples you might add departmentalization, alternative schools, self-contained classrooms, PPBS systems, reading machines, open classrooms, computer assisted instruction, listening centers, teacher centers, language labs, magnet schools, individualization, bussing, management by objectives, and on and on.

Some of these, in some settings, will work very well. The problem is that no one will know what works unless someone takes the time and effort to check. Evaluation amounts to maintaining a state of vigilance over all these new developments—*and over traditional practices as well,* since these are what the innovators hope to improve upon. Few people will dispute the need for innovative educational programs. But only when the effects of these innovations are carefully scrutinized will educators know whether they have met their own specific objectives or helped alleviate the broader educational needs they address.

Eight persuasive reasons can be put forward for taking the trouble to conduct an evaluation. They are all related to the need for making rational decisions about educational programs—decisions based on evidence. Take note of them *in case you need to convince other people* during the course of your work.

1. Evaluation can provide information needed for making specific decisions about a program—how to make it better, whether to keep it, throw it out, or expand it. Though it takes time, planning, and effort to collect such information, ultimately knowing what *results* a program or its various subcomponents are producing is the only logical basis for making effective decisions. This requires good, highly credible information.

2. Evaluation is often required by a program's funding agency. When money has been made available for a program, the people who give the money want to know about the program's results. Moreover, the local school administration, which has legal responsibility for what goes on in the schools, *should* want to know how various school programs are working out.

3. Evaluation provides a *basis of comparison* from which to judge the relative quality of good practice. You might, for instance, observe a teacher, study his methods, and find them excellent. But you might find another teacher using different methods yet producing comparable results. Similarly with programs. Different programs might all produce the same results, or one program might be outstanding. Unless you measure, you will not know the relative effects of different practices on achievement, attitudes, morale, etc. You measure because you do not know, and because you cannot know by just observing a process what outcomes it will produce.

4. *Accumulated* results from many evaluations can serve as a basis for conclusions about what sorts of programs work best, in particular settings, and under particular conditions. As many disappointed evaluators will tell you, results from a single study are seldom conclusive and as such, might influence only minor local policies or decisions. Results of the evaluation of *several* programs addressed to similar objectives, however, are likely to show trends that can be taken more seriously.

5. Evaluation is the best response to the ever-present assaults from fads and the hard-sell proponents of newfangled materials and ideas. Innovations must be tried; but if educators never find out which ones work, schools will continue to be fad-ridden, always trying innovations, but never finding out whether something good has been discarded or something wonderful discovered.

6. Evaluation is an intelligent response to controversy. An accumulation of strong data can resolve what might otherwise continue as a war of opinions.

7. Evaluation persuades people to pay attention to *data* about what the schools are doing. When people making decisions pay careful attention to educational processes and their measured results—to actual achievement data, to objectively assessed attitudes, to well-documented descriptions of the implementation of programs—then teachers and other concerned people will begin to pay attention to these kinds of information as well

8. Each time an evaluation is conducted, additional people acquire evaluation skills. There is no mystery to evaluation and no need for people to feel they are at the mercy of expensive external evaluators who have arcane skills. As more and more people involved in education become familiar with evaluation methods, educators will be better able themselves to collect information and to distinguish valuable effective innovations from expensive, ineffective fads.

What About all the Charges that Evaluation Results Are Seldom, if ever, Used?

The field of evaluation is relatively new and in a state of flux. As people have attempted to evaluate educational programs, they have encountered problems and criticisms. Though it is not within the scope of this Kit to answer all questions or reply to all criticisms leveled at the field of evaluation, one critical concern must be mentioned: the complaint that program evaluation as currently practiced is of little use. This charge is usually accompanied by one of two explanations.

1. Evaluation *methods* rely on research techniques inherited from the social sciences. These techniques are inappropriate for describing large scale, complex educational endeavors.
2. Situations where evaluations are conducted are so fraught with political interests that the results of the evaluation are unlikely to determine the decisions to be made.

Concern that the methodology of social science is not appropriate for examining educational programs

Some critics of evaluation put forth the opinion that social science methods, including design and attention to technical quality of measurements, are inappropriate to evaluation. They feel that the combined and simultaneous influence of teachers, classroom management styles, groups of students, materials, settings, etc., provide situations so full of "noise" that a signal about the effectiveness of one or the other factor will not be heard.

What is more, because of the uniqueness of the setting in which any one program occurs, it cannot be exported to another setting and expected to have the same results. The classroom is not a laboratory, critics maintain; and the investigatory tools of the laboratory are not appropriate to the classroom.

These critics are probably correct when they assert that the outcomes of most evaluations will not have the conclusiveness or generalizability of laboratory studies. But they are not intended to. Evaluations are conducted to tell specific audiences about the processes and outcomes of a particular program. The reason for using social science methods in evaluation is not to yield irrefutable, generalizable knowledge. The motivation is to find a method—any method—that makes manageable the jobs of:

- Describing what is taking place in educational programs

- Producing a description that most people will accept as accurate

Of the information-gathering and interpretation techniques which have become available to evaluators to date, standard principles of measurement and research design still come closest to meeting these requirements.

Program evaluation can make *some* contribution to the accumulation of *general* knowledge about which educational priorities work. Over time, evaluation results should begin to show a pattern. Then information from evaluations can at least put people who design educational programs a bit ahead of the game. They can work from the position of having some knowledge of what in general has worked well in the past. The ultimate aim, particularly of summative evaluation, is to help to accumulate evidence of what worked well in at least similar settings, so that *before* programs are designed, good use can be made of the information.

Concern that evaluation results are overlooked because of more pressing political interests

Some writers have expressed pessimism about the usefulness of evaluation results because of the overriding social and political motives of the people who are supposed to use evaluation results for making decisions. Ross and Cronbach[1] describe the situation this way:

> Far from supplying facts and figures to an economic man, the evaluator is furnishing arms to a combatant in a war with fluid lines of battle and transient alliances; whoever can use the evaluators to gain an inch of terrain can be expected to do so. . . . The commissioning of an evaluation . . . is rarely the product of the inquiring scientific spirit; more often it is the expression of political forces.

The political situation could hamper an evaluation in several ways. For one, it might place constraints on data collection that make accurate description of the program impossible. The sponsor could, for instance, restrict the choice of sites for data collection, regulate the use of certain designs or tests, or withhold key information. Politics could, as well, cause the evaluator's report to be ignored or his results to be misinterpreted in support of someone's point of view.

Responding to any of these situations will depend on vigilance in each unique case. Remember that your major responsibility as an evaluator is to collect good information wherever possible. Your first reaction should be to examine the circumstances of the evaluation and decide whether conforming to the press of the political context will violate your own ethics. Your next response should be to find a way to collect information that will be useful to *someone*. If the evaluation is summative and experience tells you that decisions about refunding will not be based on the evaluation, a good strategy is to submit the *pro forma* report, but *turn your attention to formative evaluation.*

---

1. Ross, L., & Cronbach, L. J. Review of the handbook of evaluation research. *Educational Researcher,* 1976, *5*(10), 9-19.

The staff of the program you are evaluating can benefit from the formative information you collect. They might need to know whether the program is on schedule or whether students are progressing as planned. In addition, you will be able to find in the minds of program planners and staff questions about how best to implement the program. Most decisions about, for instance, which materials to purchase and how to structure the school day have to be made in the absence of knowledge of what will work best. *Should a sex education course take place over one week, or should it be part of a health program which goes on for a whole semester? What proportion of the social studies course should be composed of factual information as opposed to discussion of current events? Will reading practice with an audio-machine produce better results than having children tutor one another?* You can help settle questions of this sort by subjecting them to short tests. Using an evaluation design, conduct small experiments or construct attitude survey instruments to find out about students or teacher satisfaction with a particular version of the program. If program components are receiving different emphases at different sites, investigate the relative effectiveness of these different versions of the program. If, for example, the project director decides to concentrate on increasing parent participation at two sites, and at two other sites to concentrate on teacher in-service training, you could check parent and teacher attitudes *at all four sites* to see whether different emphases seemed to have different effects. If teacher attitudes were pretty similar at all four sites, the in-service would seem to be having little impact— at least on attitudes. If parent participation, on the other hand, showed a jump at the two sites where it was emphasized, but not at the other two sites—which form a control group—then *that* effort would appear to be effective. The strategy of varying the emphasis on different program features at various sites should help the program planners become more efficient in their *internal* allocation of staff, time, effort, and money. This is a valuable and worthwhile formative service.

To summarize, writers on the topic of evaluation often express disappointment that evaluation results are *not used.* It is true that evaluation studies rarely form the sole basis upon which decisions are made and that political concerns, as often as not, direct the course of action. This disappointment is alleviated somewhat, however, if one looks at evaluation information as intended to constitute only one source among many which can influence decisions, guide policy, or influence the lives of programs. To the extent that the information is well collected, credible and consistent with on-going theories of what works, the information will be heard and used according to the audience's aims in collecting it.

Why Use Control Groups and Evaluation Designs?

Whether you are a formative or a summative evaluator, what you will be able to say about the program will depend to a large extent upon the *design* you choose for your evaluation. *An evaluation design is a plan of which groups will take part in the evaluation and when measurements will be made on these groups.*

You probably already know a bit about design—that it involves assignment of students or classrooms to programs, and to comparison or control groups. The purpose of this discussion is to present you with the logic underlying the need for good design in evaluations where you want to show that there is a relationship between program activities and outcomes.

First consider the common *before and after* design. In the typical situation, a new program has been instituted and an evaluation planned. The evaluator administers a pretest at the beginning of the program, and at the end of the program, a posttest as in the following examples:

- *A new district-wide mathematics program is evaluated. The California Achievement Test is administered in September and again in May.*
- *An individual school has set itself the goal of increasing parent participation in a bilingual education project. The evaluator observes and records parent attendance at planning meetings at the beginning of the first semester and then again at the end.*
- *An objective of a state mandated junior high school reorganization project is to increase student enjoyment of school. Students fill in a questionnaire at the beginning of the year and then again at the end of the year.*

Any of these situations can be represented, as in Figure 2, by

$$O \qquad\qquad X \qquad\qquad O$$

The first **O** stands for Observation—at the beginning of the year or at the beginning of the program. Thus **O** was an arithmetic pretest in the math project, a count of parents in the bilingual program, a questionnaire to students in the last example.

X means Program **X**, the one that was implemented to bring about improvement in whatever **O** measures. **X** might be new materials, a new way of organizing, or a new set of procedures. It could even be the *old* way of doing things, though it seldom is. The program, **X**, is what is being evaluated.

The second **O** is the final observation or "posttest." This is the *outcome* measure for the program. Results on the outcome measure are usually scrutinized to determine whether the program did what it was supposed to do. This is where the before-and-after design leaves the evaluation vulnerable to challenge. It fails to answer two important questions:

1. How good are the results? Could they have been better? Would they have been the same if the program had *not* been carried out?
2. Was it the program that brought about these results or was it something else?

Figure 2. Diagram of the sequence of events in the before-and-after, pretest-posttest evaluation design

Consider the following situation. A new reading program has been put into effect at Lincoln Middle School. Ms. Pryor, the principal, wants to assess the quality of the program by examining students' grade equivalent scores from a standardized reading test given in September and then again in May. She notes that the sixth grade average was 5.4 in September and 6.5 in May. She attempts to judge the value of the new reading program based on this pretest-posttest information.

RESULTS ON STATE READING TEST— 6TH GRADES		
READING PROGRAM	SEPT. PRETEST (G.E.)	MAY POSTTEST (G.E.)
SUNNYDATE LEARNING ASSOCIATES	5.4	6.5

The middle school students in the example have shown a considerable gain in reading from pretest to posttest—1.1 grade equivalent points. On the other hand, they are still not reading at grade level. Therefore Ms. Pryor must ask herself, *How good are these results?* The answer depends, of course, on the children and the conditions in the school and home. For some groups, this would represent great progress; for others, it would indicate serious difficulties in the program.

How can Ms. Pryor find out what progress she should expect from her sixth graders? The pretest tells her something—the sixth-graders were six months behind in September, and they ended up only four months behind in May.

Perhaps without the new program they would have ended up five months behind. Or perhaps they would have done better with the old program! In order to know what difference the program made, she needs to know *how the students would have scored without the program.* One solution is to look at results on the same test from sixth graders in previous years. This solution, however, leaves open the possibility that this particular class is different.

Ms. Pryor cannot, in fact, judge the quality of the sixth grade program solely on the basis of the pre- and posttests. She can guess at the answer, but she cannot say for sure.

Ms. Pryor has another problem in interpreting her results. She cannot even show that the gains she *did* get on the posttest were *brought about by* the reading program. Perhaps there were other changes that occurred in the school or among the students this year—a drop in class size, or a larger number of parents volunteering to tutor, or the miraculous absence of difficult" children who demanded teacher time and distracted the class. Many influences might cause the learning situation to alter from year to year.

Ms. Pryor, of course, could have ruled out most of these explanations of her results by using a control group. First, two *randomly* formed groups would have been assigned at the beginning of the year to either the new reading program or to another semester of the old one. Before the program began, both groups would have been pretested. At the end of the year, the groups would be posttested using the same reading test.

The diagram for a two-groups randomized design appears in Figure 3. This *true control group* design turns an evaluation into a source of valid and valuable information. If Ms. Pryor had used this design, her evaluation question would have been:

Were the posttest scores of the experimental group— those who received the new reading program—better than those for the control group, who got the old reading program?

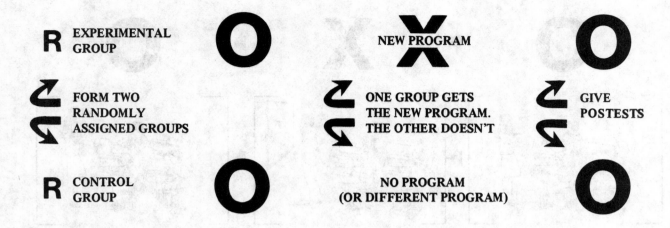

Figure 3. Diagram of the sequence of events in the true control group design

Because the two groups were initially equivalent, the scores of the control group would show how the new program students would have scored if they had not received the new program:

PROGRAM	PRETEST	POSTTEST
SUNNYDATE (X)	5.4	6.5
OLD PROGRAM (CONTROL GROUP)	5.4	6.1

But was it the new program that brought about the improvement, or was it some other factor? Using a true control group design, Ms. Pryor can discount the influence of other factors as long as these factors have probably also affected the control group. If, for instance, some students had had an enriched nursery school program that got them off to a good start in reading, the *random assignment* should have spread these students fairly evenly between the two groups. If more parents were helping in the school, this should have benefitted both groups equally. If this year's sixth grade was generally quieter, with fewer difficult children, this should have affected both the experimental and control groups equally. Ms. Pryor does not even have to know what all the factors might have been. By randomly assigning the two groups, the influence of various factors affecting the reading achievement of the two groups is likely to be equalized. Then differences observed in outcomes can be attributed to the one factor that has been made deliberately different: the reading program.

Though much maligned as impractical, the true control group design produces such credible and interpretable results that it should at least be considered an ideal to be approximated when evaluation studies are planned.[2] The design is valuable because it provides a comparative basis from which to examine the results of the program in question. It helps to rule out the challenges of potential skeptics that good attitudes or improved achievement were brought about by factors other than the program.

In Ms. Pryor's situation, the control group would have received the old reading program. Actually, the control group might have done several things as Figure 4 shows. For instance, it could have been given *another new program,* a program that Ms. Pryor considered a potential competitor to the new reading program—one she might have considered adopting. In this way, the evaluation would have been converted into a true *consumer test* informing Ms. Pryor which of two new programs gives better results or is easiest to implement. Sometimes a control group that receives *no program at all* can provide results with which you can compare the program's effects. A no-program control group is especially helpful when evaluating programs that aim toward promoting attitudes like self-esteem or teaching skills such as "reading readiness" that might "just develop" without a program.

It is not always easy to convince people that random assignment and experimentation are good things; and of course you must make decisions that are consistent with the opinions of your audience. When prescribing methods for planning evaluations, the Kit procedures, therefore, take into account possible objections of school or community members.

---

2. Actually, true control group designs *have* been used in evaluation of many educational and social programs. A list of 141 of them, with references, is contained in Boruch, R. F. Bibliography: Illustrative randomized field experiments for program planning and evaluation. *Evaluation,* 1974, *2*(1), 83-87.

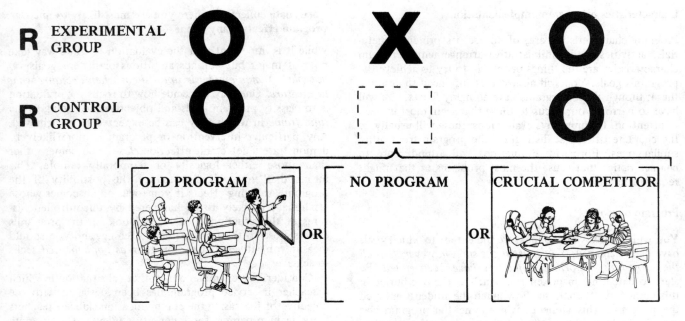

Figure 4. Alternative versions of the true control group design showing differences in what the control group experiences

The best strategy is to consider using a design for planning the administration of each measurement instrument you will use. Consider a randomized design first. If this is not possible, then look for a *non-equivalent control group*—people as much like the program group as possible but who will receive no program or a different program. Or try to use a *time-series design* as a basis for comparison: find relevant data about the *former* performance of program groups or of past groups in the same setting. Only if none of these designs is possible should you abandon using a design. An evaluation that can say "Compared to such-and-such, *this* is what the program produced" is more interpretable than one like Ms. Pryor's that simply reports scores in a vacuum.

How Does an Evaluator Decide What To Measure?

An evaluator might decide to measure an infinite number of things: smiles per second, math achievement, time scheduled for reading, district innovativeness, number of students bringing materials to class, fathers' occupations, number of parents attending school meetings, self-concept, and on and on. The term *to measure* is used here in its broadest sense: it means *to record for the purpose of summarizing and reporting.*

Carrying out an evaluation in any area of education is a matter of collecting evidence to demonstrate the effects of a program or one of its subcomponents. The program's objectives, your role, and the audience's motives will help you to make *gross* decisions about what to look at. Four general aspects of a program might be measured as part of your evaluation:

- Context characteristics
- Student characteristics
- Characteristics of program implementation
- Program outcomes

Context characteristics

Educational programs take place within a setting or context—a framework of constraints within which a program must operate. The context characteristics are the *givens* for a program—the situation in which a program finds itself, so to speak. They might include such things as class size, style of leadership in the school, district organization, time frame within which the program must operate, number of classrooms per site, or school budget. It is especially important to get accurate information about aspects of the context that you suspect might affect the success of the program. If, for example, you suspect that programs like the one you are evaluating might be effective under one style of school governance but not under another kind, you should try to assess leadership style at the various sites to explore that possibility.

Student characteristics

Student characteristics include such things as age, sex, socioeconomic status, language dominance, ability, attendance record, and attitudes. It may sometimes be important to see if a program shows different effects with different groups of students. For example, if teachers say the least well-behaved students seem to like the program but the best behaved students do not like it, you would want to collect ratings of "well-behavedness" prior to the program and examine your results to detect whether these different reactions did indeed occur.

Characteristics of program implementation

Program characteristics are, of course, its principal materials, activities, and administrative arrangements. Program characteristics are the things people *do* to try to achieve the program's goals. You will almost certainly need to describe these; though most programs have so many facets, you will have to narrow your focus to those that seem most in need of attention. In summative evaluations, these will usually be the characteristics that distinguish the program from other similar ones. Formative evaluations will attend more to characteristics that cause the most problems or that might require alteration.

Program outcomes

You will usually want to measure the extent to which goals have been achieved. *You must make sure, however, that all the program's important objectives have been stated.* Be alert to detecting unspoken goals such as the one buried in this comment: "I could see how much the students enjoyed the program. This alone convinced me the program was good." At least in the eyes of the person who said this, enjoyment was a program goal, or a highly valued outcome, whether or not this was so stated in program plans. You also need to ask whether outcomes are immediately measurable. Some hoped-for outcomes may be so long-range that only a study of many years' duration could establish that they had occurred. This would be the case, for example, with goals such as "increased job satisfaction in adult life" or "a life-long love of books."

The evaluator should in general focus the evaluation on announced goals, but should be careful to include the possible wishes of the program's larger constituency—for example, the community—in formulating the yardsticks against which the program will be held accountable.

Beyond these general guidelines, decisions about exactly *what* information to collect will be situation-specific. Every program has distinctive goals; and every situation makes available unique kinds of data. Though there is no simple way to decide what specific information to collect, or what variables to look at, there are some rules of thumb you can follow:

1. Focus data collection where you are most likely to uncover program effects if any occur.
2. Try to collect a variety of information.
3. Try to think of clever—and credible—ways to detect achievement of program objectives.
4. Collect information to show that the program at least has done no harm.
5. Measure what you think members of the audience will look for when they receive your report.
6. Try to measure things that will advance the development of educational theory.

Use of each of these pointers is discussed below.

Focus data collection where you are most likely to uncover program effects if any occur

While it is important that the evaluation in some way take note of major but perhaps ambitious or distant goals, *do not place major emphasis upon them when deciding what to measure.* One way to decide how to focus the evaluation is to classify program goals and objectives according to the *time frame* in which they can be expected to be achieved. Any particular intervention or program is more likely to demonstrate a detectable effect on *close-in* outcomes rather than those either logically or temporally remote. This means that you will also reduce the possibility of the program's showing effects if you focus on outcomes whose attainment is likely to be hampered by uncontrolled features of the situation. You should look for the program's effects close to the time of their teaching, and you should measure objectives that the program *as implemented* seeks to achieve.

Consider, for example, a hypothetical situation in which a teacher in-service program has been designed with the objective of increasing the communication skills of teachers working in programs for inner-city students. The program was instituted in order eventually to accomplish these primary goals:

- To decrease teacher absenteeism and early retirement because of high pressure on the job
- To encourage congenial interpersonal relationships among teachers and students
- To decrease the number of student disciplinary referrals
- To decrease the number of citizen complaints about the handling of students by the teachers

In evaluating this program, you could measure the amount of teacher absences and the number of hostile teacher-student encounters occurring before, during, and after the program; the number of students sent for disciplinary action; and the incidence of community complaints. These, after all, are measures reflecting the program's impact on its major objectives.

There is a problem with basing the evaluation *solely* on these objectives, however. *Judgments of the quality of the program will then be based only on the program's apparent effect on these outcomes.* While these *are* the major outcomes of interest, they are remote effects likely to come about through a long chain of events which the teacher in-service program has only begun. A better evaluation would include attention to whether teachers learned anything from the in-service training program itself, or whether they displayed the classroom behaviors the in-service was designed to produce.

In general, since there are various ways in which a program can affect its participants, one of the evaluator's most valuable contributions might be to determine at what *level* the program has had an effect. Think of a program as potentially affecting people in three different ways:

1. *At minimum, it can make members of the target group aware that its services are available.* Prospective partici-

pants can simply learn that the program is taking place and that an effort is being made to address their educational needs. In some situations, demonstrating that the target audience has been informed that the program is accessible to them might be important. This will be the case particularly with programs that rely on voluntary enrollment, such as life-long learning programs, a venereal disease education program, or outreach programs for handicapped and special children. Evaluation of these kinds of programs will require a check on the quality of their publicity.

2. *A program can impart useful information.* It might be the case that a program's most valuable outcome is the conveyance of information to some group. Learning, of course, is the major objective to *most* educational programs. Although most programs aim toward loftier goals than just the receipt of information, attention should not be diverted from assessing whether its less ambitious effects occurred. In the teacher in-service example, for instance, it would be important to show that teachers have become more aware of the problems and life experiences of minority students. If you are unable to show an impact on their *behavior,* you can at least show that the program has taught them something.

3. *A program can actually influence changes in behavior.* The most difficult evaluation to undertake is one that looks for the influence of a program on people's day to day behavior. While behavior and attitude change are at the top of the list of many program objectives, actually determining whether such changes have occurred often requires more effort than the evaluator can muster. You will, of course, be interested in at least keeping tabs on whether the program is achieving some of its grander goals. Consider yourself warned, however, that the probability of a program showing a powerful behavioral effect might be minimal.

Try to collect a variety of information

Three good strategies will help you do this. First, try to find useful information which is going to be collected anyhow. Find out which tests are given as part of the program or routinely in the setting; look at the teachers' plans for assessment; look at records from the program or at reports, journals, and logs which are to be kept. Check to see whether evidence of the achievement of some of the program's objectives can be inferred from these.

Another good way to increase the amount of information you collect is by finding someone to collect information for you. You might persuade teachers to establish record keeping systems that will benefit both your evaluation and their instruction. You might hire someone such as a student from a local high school or college to collect information. Perhaps you can even persuade a graduate student seeking a topic for a research study to choose one whose data collection will coincide with your evaluation.

Finally, a good way to increase the kinds of information you can collect is to use sampling procedures. They will cut down the time you must spend administering and interpreting any one measure. Choosing representative sites,

events, or participants on which to focus, or randomly sampling groups for testing, will usually produce information as credible to your audiences as if you had looked at the entire population of people served.

Collecting a variety of information gives you the advantage of presenting a thorough look at the program. It also gives you a good chance of finding indicators of significant program effects and of collecting evidence to corroborate some of your shakier findings.

Besides accumulating a *breadth* of information about the program, you might decide to conduct *case studies* to lend your picture of the program greater depth and complexity. The case study evaluator, interested in the broad range of events and relationships which affect participants in the program, chooses to examine closely a particular case—that is, a school, a classroom, a particular group, or even an individual. This method enables you to present the proportionate influence of the program among the myriad other factors influencing the actions and feelings of the people under study. Case studies will give your audience a strong notion of the flavor of the activities which constituted the program and the way in which these activities fit into the daily experiences of participants.

Try to think of clever—and credible—ways to detect achievement of program objectives

Suppose in the teacher in-service example discussed earlier, it turns out that teacher absenteeism has remained unchanged and that the number of disciplinary referrals has diminished only slightly. These findings make the program look ineffective.

It might be the case, however, that though teachers have continued to send students to the office, they are discussing problems more often among themselves, reading more about minority groups, and talking more often with parents. Perhaps the *content* of referral slips has changed. Rather than noting a student's offense by a curt remark, maybe teachers are now sending diagnostic and suggestive information to the school office.

A little thought to the more mundane ways in which the program might affect participants could lead you to collect key information about program effects. A good way to uncover nonobvious but important indicators of program impact is to ask participants during the course of the evaluation about changes they have seen occurring. Where an informal report uncovers an intriguing effect, check the generality of this person's perception by means of a quick questionnaire or a test to a sample of students. You should, incidentally, try to keep a little money in the evaluation budget to finance such *ad hoc* data gathering.

Collect information to show that the program at least has done no harm

In deciding what to measure, keep in mind the possible objections of skeptics or of the program's critics. A common objection is that the time spent taking part in the program might have been better spent pursuing another activity. Sometimes the evaluation of a program, therefore, will need to attend to the issue of whether students or participants, by spending time in the program, may have missed some other important educational experience. This is likely to be the case with programs which remove students from the usual learning environment to take part in special activities. "Pull-out" programs of this kind are often directed toward students with special needs—either enrichment or remediation. You may need to show, for instance, that students who take part in a speech therapy program during reading time, have not suffered in their reading achievement. Similarly, you may need to show that an accelerated junior high school science program has not actually prevented students from learning science concepts usually taught at this level.

Related to the problem of demonstrating that students have not missed opportunities for learning is the requirement that you also show the program did no actual harm. For instance, attitude programs aimed at human relations skills or people's self-perceptions could conceivably go awry and provoke neuroses. Where your audience is likely to express concern about these matters, you should anticipate the concern by looking for these effects yourself.

Measure what you think members of the audience will look for when they receive your report

Try to get to know the audience who will receive your evaluation information. Find out what they most want to know. Are they, for instance, more concerned about the proper implementation of the program than about its outcomes? A parent advisory group, for instance, might wish to see an open classroom functioning in the school. They may be more concerned with the installation of the program than with student achievement, at least during the first year of operation. In this case, your evaluation should pay more attention to measures of program implementation than to outcomes although progress reports will be appropriate as well. If you get to know your audience, you will realize that, for instance, Mr. Johnson on the school board always wants to know about integration or interpersonal understanding; or the foundation that supplied funding is mainly concerned with potential job skills. Visualize members of the audience reading or hearing your report; try to put yourself in their place. Think of the questions you would ask the evaluator if you were they.

Try to measure things that will advance the development of educational theory

Evaluators who work in academic settings are just about always trying to do this. Educational theories are made up of *process models*—descriptions of the relationship between program activities, or processes, and program outcomes. A process model allows for this kind of description: "Programs that contain Factors X (program, teacher, or student characteristics), are likely to produce Outcome A (an attitude, a skill, or behavior)." Designing evaluations with the development and testing of process models in mind serves an important function: It provides information that can be used eventually for program planning and development. The current state of knowledge in education makes it necessary that programs be evaluated *post hoc*—that is,

after someone's best guesses have put together a program. To the extent that a process model can be identified—ideas of what works in which settings—some of the guess work can be eliminated from the design of educational programs.

The evaluator using a process model approach first develops a detailed explanation of how the program is supposed to work. The planners of any well thought out program will be able to provide such an explanation. The evaluator then identifies checkpoints at which information can be collected to see if the program really has been implemented the way its planners claim it should be. This information will reflect whether the factors that are supposed to bring about good outcomes are indeed present. The evaluator then examines the program outcomes—achievement, attitudes, etc. If a good design has been used, perhaps with a control group or time series data, then the evaluator can build a fairly strong case that the critical characteristics comprising the program have at least in this case been associated with certain outcomes.

Consider an example of how development and testing of a process model might take place. Suppose that as one component of a remedial math program a room has been set aside in which parent volunteer aides will tutor students who are having particular problems. Program funds pay for maintenance, furnishings, and materials in this room. *It is assumed that the parent-aide room contributes to the goal of math remediation.* The evaluator, hoping to measure in accordance with the testing of this still-quite-general but naisent process model, interviews program staff. She wants to know what they consider to be the *critical characteristics* of the program, that is, the set of materials and activities which will bring about increased math achievement in the target students. Using the information provided by program planners and staff, she creates the following, more mature, but still only tentative, process model with checkpoints indicated by questions:

- Parents will know of the existence of the parent-aide room (Do they?) and know that they will be welcome there to serve as tutors (Do parents feel this way?).
- Parents will visit the room (Can they, or are they at work when the room is open? How many parents do actually visit?).
- Parents will receive *instruction* about how to help the children (Do they? Is this effective instruction? Do parents feel at the conclusion of instruction that they are well qualified to tutor?) and will apply this instruction with the children whom they will tutor (Do they apply the instructions? How much time is spent on instruction, and how much on other activities?).
- This will improve children's math skills (Does parent instruction help improve children's math skills? Is parent help given with enough consistency to make a difference?).

As you can see, simply spelling out the desired processes—that is, the chain of events that links math remediation to the parent-aide room—suggests a variety of checks that can be made to see if the process is working, and if not, where it is breaking down. The job of a formative evaluator, you may surmise, will be to make sure the program stays on course and to look for areas where the process model has broken down.

The job of summative evaluator is more often to explain, document, and describe how well the process model seems to have worked. A summative evaluation that is focused on a process model and also employs a good design constitutes a research study and is subsequently publishable. Its results are important to the educational community at large.

For Further Reading

Anderson, S. B. Educational compensation and evaluation: A critique. In J. C. Stanley (Ed.), *Compensatory education for children ages two to eight.* Baltimore, MD: John Hopkins University Press, 1973.

Ball, S., & Anderson, S. B. *Practices in program evaluation: A survey and some case studies.* Princeton, NJ: Educational Testing Service, 1975.

Bennett, C. A., & Lumsdaine, A. A. (Eds.) *Evaluation and experiment.* New York: Academic Press, 1975.

Borich, G. D. (Ed.) *Evaluating educational programs and products.* Englewood Cliffs, NJ: Educational Technology Publications, 1974.

Boruch, R. F. Bibliography: Illustrative randomized field experiments for program planning and evaluation. *Evaluation,* 1974, *2*(1), 83-87.

Campbell, D. T. Reforms as experiments. In C. H. Weiss (Ed.), *Evaluating action programs: Readings in social action and education.* Boston: Allyn & Bacon, 1972.

Cook, T. D., Appleton, H., Conner, R., Shaffer, A., Tomkin, G., & Weber, S. J. *Sesame street revisited: A case study in evaluative research.* New York: Russell Sage Foundation, 1972.

Cooley, W. H., & Lohnes, P. R. *Evaluation research in education: Theory, principles, and practice.* New York: Irvington, 1976.

Edwards, W., Guttentag, M., & Snapper, K. A decision-theoretic approach to evaluation research. In E. L. Struening & M. Guttentag (Eds.), *Handbook of evaluation research.* Volume 1. Beverly Hills, CA: Sage Publications, 1975.

Glass, G. V. *Evaluation studies review annual.* Volume 1. Beverly Hills: Sage Publications, 1976.

Guba, E. G., & Stufflebeam, D. L. *Evaluation: The Process of stimulating, aiding, and abetting insightful action.* Monograph Series in Reading Education, No. 1. Bloomington: Indiana University, 1970.

Guttentag, M., & Struening, E. L. *Handbook of evaluation research.* Volume 2. Beverly Hills: Sage Publications, 1975.

Levin, H. M. Cost effectiveness analysis in evaluation research. In M. Guttentag and E. L. Struening (Eds.), *Handbook of Evaluation Research.* Volume 2. Beverly Hills: Sage Publications, 1975.

MacDonald, B. *Evaluation and the control of education.* Norwich, England: Center for Applied Research in Education, University of East Anglia, 1974.

Provus, M. *Discrepancy evaluation.* Berkeley, CA: McCutchan, 1971.

Provus, M. Toward a state system of evaluation. *Journal of Research and Development in Education,* 1972, *5*(4), 87-96.

Riecken, H. W., & Boruch, R. F. (Eds.). *Social experimentation: A method for planning and evaluating social intervention.* New York: Academic Press, 1974.

Rippey, R. M. (Ed.). *Studies in transactional evaluation.* Berkeley, CA: McCutchan, 1973.

Scriven, M. The methodology of evaluation. In American Educational Research Association, *Perspectives of curriculum evaluation.* Chicago: McNally, 1967.

Stake, R. E. The countenance of educational evaluation. *Teachers College Record,* 1967, *68,* 523-540.

Stake, R. E. Toward a technology for the evaluation of educational programs. In American Educational Research Association, *Perspectives of curriculum evaluation.* Chicago: McNally, 1967.

Stufflebeam, D. L., Foley, W. J., Gephart, W. J., Guba, E. G., Hammond, R. L., Merriman, H. O., & Provus, M. M. *Educational evaluation and decision-making.* Itasca, IL: Peacock, 1971.

Suchman, E. A. *Evaluative research: Principles and practice in public service and social action programs.* New York: Russell Sage Foundation, 1967.

Weiss, C. H. (Ed.). *Evaluating action programs: Readings in social action and education.* Boston: Allyn & Bacon, 1972.

Worthen, B. R., & Sanders, J. S. *Educational evaluation: Theory and practice.* Worthington, OH: Chas. A. Jones, 1973.

How to Play the Role of Formative Evaluator

As the political constraints on most summative evaluations have become more apparent, and as lay planning groups have become involved in making decisions about school programs, interest has increased in formative evaluation. The formative evaluator is essentially the member of a program-planning-and-revision team who is charged with the task of collecting information about quality of implementation, attitudes, and achievement at various sites so that a program can be improved as it develops. This chapter presents a description of the many facets of the role of formative program evaluator and outlines the responsibilities and activities associated with the job. Since the tasks of the formative evaluator change with the context, it is inappropriate to prescribe what this person *must do*. Rather, the chapter will describe her *role* with regard to the program and suggest some of the activities in which she *might* become involved.

Whatever their situation, formative evaluators do share a set of common goals. Their major aim, of course, is to ensure that the program be implemented as effectively as possible. The formative evaluator watches over the program, alert both for problems and for good ideas that can be shared. The goal of bringing about modifications for a program's improvement carries with it four subgoals:

- To determine, in company with program planners and staff, what sorts of information about the program will be collected and shared and what decisions will be based on this information

- To assure that the program's goals and objectives, and the major characteristics of its implementation, have been well thought out and carefully recorded

- To collect data at program sites about what the program looks like in operation and about the program's effects on attitudes and achievement

- To report this information clearly and to help the staff plan related program modifications

This chapter discusses in detail various ways to accomplish each of these tasks. Chapter 3 then presents four Step-by-Step Guides—one for completing each of the activities outlined here. In order to communicate the interpersonal character of formative evaluation, the word *agenda* is substituted for *goal*. *Agenda* refers not only to a goal, but also to a plan for a meeting. Since as formative evaluator you will need to meet frequently with planners and staff, the tasks you perform to accomplish each goal might well provide topics for discussion at several meetings.

Activities of the formative evaluator, then, are aimed toward accomplishing four agendas corresponding to his major goals. These are:

Agenda A. Set the Boundaries of the Evaluation

Agenda B. Prepare a Program Statement

Agenda C. Monitor Program Implementation and the Achievement of Program Objectives

Agenda D. Report and Confer with Planners and Staff

You might think of each agenda as a set of information-gathering activities culminating in one or more meetings where decisions are made about the next information-gathering cycle. Although it would be logical to perform the tasks subsumed under each agenda in the sequence presented above, you will likely find yourself working at two or more agendas simultaneously or cycling back through them again and again. This will be particularly the case with Agendas C and D; you might collect, report, and discuss implementation and progress data many times during the course of the evaluation. Meetings with staff are also likely to involve more than one agenda.

Agenda A: Set the Boundaries of the Evaluation

Your first job will be to delineate the scope of the evaluation by sketching out with the program staff a description of *what your tasks will be*. This first plan might result in a contract describing what you will do for the staff, as well as the responsibility *they* will assume to help you gather information, and to act upon what you report.

As soon as you have hung up your telephone, having spoken with someone requesting a formative evaluation, you are confronted with Agenda A. It could be that the person asked you outright to help with project improvement. Or perhaps you *chose* to focus on providing formative information to the project after having been given the job of summative evaluator or an ambiguous evaluation role. It could be as well that you started out as one of the program's planners and that your role as formative evaluator is simply a "change of hats," a shift from your previous responsibilities.

Initial contacts

If you have been asked to assist in monitoring an on-going program, you should find out as much as possible about the program before meeting with the staff and planners, your formative audience. A recommended first activity is calling a friend familiar with this or similar programs. In addition to sharing basic information, he may be able to help you anticipate problems with the evaluation or with developing a good relationship with staff.

By all means ask the program planners for documents related to funding and development or adoption of the program. These documents might include an RFP (Request for Proposals) issued by the funding source when it first offered money for such programs, the program plan or proposal, and program descriptions written for other reasons such as public relations. Use these documents to form an initial general understanding of what the program is supposed to look like, what its goals might be, and particularly, what shape the evaluation might take.

In addition, it may be worth your while to quickly check the educational literature to see what, if anything, has recently been written about programs like the one in question, or about specific components—say, commercial curriculum materials—that planners intend to use. You may even find earlier evaluations of this or similar programs.

Encourage cooperation

For whatever reason you undertake formative evaluation, the first step will be to establish a working relationship with the program staff. Since formative evaluation depends on sharing information informally, one of the outcomes of Agenda A should be the establishment of groundwork for a trusting, insider's relationship with the staff and planners. If your evaluation has been commissioned by the program staff itself, establishing trust will be easier than if the contractor is an external agency, perhaps the state or federal government. In the latter case, you will start out an *outsider.* Program personnel will suspect that you are taking an evaluative look at their program for someone else. To avoid ending up in an adversary position against a defensive program staff, you will need to convince the staff that your primary allegiance is to help *them* discover how to optimize program implementation and outcomes. You might describe the form that your outside reporting will take and allow the staff a chance to review your external reports. You might explore, as well, the possibility of taking an outright advocacy position in your report to the sponsor. Whenever it seems necessary, you might also guarantee that information shared for the purpose of *internal* program review and improvement will be kept confidential. An important way to gain the confidence of program personnel is to *make yourself useful* from the very beginning, efficiently collecting the information they need or would like to have.

Elicit information from the staff

While mutual trust must be worked out gradually, some more practical aspects of your role can be negotiated during a single meeting. Agenda A requires that you and the project staff decide together what you will *do* for them.

If you arrive early during program development, you may find that the staff needs help in identifying program goals and choosing related instructional materials, activities, etc. Even after the program has begun, they may still be planning. Regardless of the state of program development

when you begin, you should help the staff outline what they consider to be the primary characteristics of the program, highlighting those which they consider fixed and those which they consider *changeable enough to be the focus of formative evaluation.*

It is important to get a clear picture of the attitudes of teachers and planners, particularly concerning their *commitment to change,* that is, the extent to which they are willing to use the information you collect to make modifications in the program. Though neither you nor they will be able to anticipate beforehand precisely what actions will follow upon the information you report, you should get some idea of the extent to which the staff is willing to alter the program.

In general, laying the groundwork for your formative evaluation means asking the planners and staff such questions as:

- Which parts of the program do you consider its most distinctive characteristics, those that make it unique among programs of its kind?
- Which aspects of the program do you think wield greatest influence in producing the attitudes or achievement the program is supposed to bring about?
- What components would you *like* the program to have which it does not contain currently? Might we try some of these on a temporary basis?
- Which parts of the program as it looks currently are most troublesome, most controversial, or most in need of vigilant attention?
- On *what* are you most and least willing, or constrained, to spend additional money? Would you be willing or *could* you, for instance, purchase another mathematics series? Can you hire additional personnel or consultants?
- Where would you be most agreeable to *cutbacks?* Can you, for instance, remove personnel? If the audio-visual learning equipment were found to be ineffective, would you eliminate it? Which books, materials, and other program components would you be willing to delete? Would you be willing to scrap the program as it currently looks and start over?
- How much administrative or staff reorganization will the situation tolerate? Can you change people's roles? Can you add to staff, say, by bringing in volunteers? Can you move people—teachers, even students—from location to location permanently or temporarily? Can you reassign students to different programs or groups?
- How much instructional and curricular change will you tolerate in the program beyond its current state? Would you be willing to delete, add, or alter the program's objectives? To what extent would you be willing to change books, materials, and other program components? Are you willing to rewrite lessons?

The objective behind asking these questions is *not* to record a detailed description of the program. This will be done under Agenda B. Rather, the purpose is to uncover particularly maleable aspects of the program. The best way to find out about the staff's commitment to change is to ask these hard questions early. A dedicated staff that has worked diligently to plan the program will likely have in mind a point beyond which it will not go in making modifications. You should locate that point, and choose the program features you will monitor accordingly.

Another important consideration in uncovering staff loyalties and attitudes is their commitment to a particular *philosophy of education.* If they are adopting a canned program, this philosophy probably motivated their choice. Staff members developing a program from scratch may also subscribe to a single motivating philosophy. However, you may find it poorly articulated or even unclearly evidenced in the program. In this case, you can create a basis for future decision-making by helping the staff to clarify and put into practice what their philosophy says.

If you can help the staff outline areas of the program where modifications are likely to be either necessary or possible, then they can begin to delineate the parts of the program whose effectiveness should be scrutinized. This will, in turn, suggest the kinds of information they will need. If the program is based on canned curricula which will simply be *installed,* or on materials not expressly designed for the type of program in question, then what you can change will be restricted. In this case you should focus on how best to make materials or procedures fit the context.

Example. A group of language arts teachers in a large high school decided that an alarming number of ninth-grade students were unable to read at a level sufficient to appreciate the literary content of their courses. They decided to institute a tutoring program in which twelfth graders would spend three forty-five minute periods a week reading literary selections with ninth graders. The aim of the project was to improve the ninth-graders' reading as well as to introduce them to English literature. The reading selections used for this program were from *Pathways to English,* a popular ninth-grade anthology; the district budget did not include funds to purchase reading materials for secondary students.

The school's assistant principal, Al Washington, monitored closely the progress of the tutoring program. After only three months had passed, he noticed some disappointment among the initially enthusiastic teachers. Their informal assessments of the reading of tutees had convinced them that little progress had been made. Although the students enjoyed the tutoring experience, they were not learning to read. The teachers asked Mr. Washington to evaluate the program with an eye toward suggesting changes in the materials or the tutoring arrangements that would help the ninth graders with their reading. Mr. Washington carefully examined the *Pathways to English* text, observed tutoring sessions, and interviewed tutors and tutees. From this information he drew three conclusions about the program and offered suggestions for remedial action: (1) the vocabulary in *Pathways to English* was too difficult for the ninth graders, so each unit should be preceded by a vocabulary drill using a standard procedure that would be taught to tutors; (2) ninth graders were *listening* more than reading, so tutoring sessions should be restructured to follow a "you read to me and I read to you" format in which twelfth and ninth graders alternate reading passages; (3) the program as constituted gave ninth graders no feedback about their progress in either reading or literary appreciation—therefore, the teachers should write short unit tests in vocabulary, comprehension, and appreciation.

In the case where a wholly new program is being developed, you will want to identify the most promising sorts of modifications that can be made within existing budget limitations. You may find it most useful to concentrate on helping the staff select from among several alternatives the most popular or effective form the program can take.

Example. KDKC, an educational television station serving a large city, received a contract from the federal government to produce 13 segments of a series about intercultural understanding directed at middle grade students. The objective of the series would be to promote appreciation of diverse cultures by depicting life in the home countries of the major cultural groups comprising the population of the United States.

The producers of the series set out at once to assemble the programs based on the format of popular primary grade programs: the central characters living in a culturally diverse neighborhood converse with each other about their respective backgrounds. These conversations lead into vignettes—filmed and animated—depicting life and culture in different countries. Some members of the production staff, however, suggested that a program format suitable for the primary grades may "bomb" with older students. "How do we know," they asked, "what interests 10- and 11-year olds?" They suggested two formats which might be more effective: a fast action adventure spy story with documentary interludes and a dramatic program focusing on teen-age students traveling in different countries.

To test these intriguing notions, the producer called on Dr. Schwartz, a professor of Child Development. Dr. Schwartz, however, had to admit that he was not sure what would most interest middle grade students either. Since the federal grant included funds for planning, Dr. Schwartz suggested that the producer assemble three pilot shows presenting basically the same knowledge via each of the three major formats being considered and then show these to students in the target age group, assessing what they learned and their enjoyment. The producer liked the idea of letting an experiment determine the form of the programs and agreed to allow Dr. Schwartz to conduct the studies, serving as a formative evaluator.

Outline for the staff the services you can provide

In accomplishing Agenda A, you will want to convey to the project staff and planners a description of what you can and cannot do for them within the constraints of your abilities, time, and budget. You should let them know the sorts of choices you will have to make based on staff preferences and likely future circumstances. It is also desirable that you frankly discuss both your areas of greatest competence and those in which you lack expertise. The staff should know in what ways you believe you can be of most benefit to the program as well as how the program might profit from the services of a consultant who could handle matters outside your competence.

Although you should have an evaluation plan in mind before you meet with staff and planners, let your audience have the opportunity to select from among several options; present your preferences as recommendations, and negotiate the general form your evaluation services will take. Try not to become enmeshed in details too early. You need only agree initially on an outline of your evaluation responsibilities. As the program develops, these plans could easily change. When describing the service you might perform, list the kinds of questions you will try to answer—about academic progress, effective use of materials, proper and timely implementation of activities, adequacy of administrative procedures, and changes in attitudes. Describe, as well, the supporting data you will gather to back up depictions of program events and outcomes.

If you feel that the situation will accommodate the use of a particular evaluation design, then propose it and describe how designs increase the interpretability of data. In cases where you note controversy over the inclusion of a program component, or where there exists a set of instructional alternatives without a persuasive reason to favor any one of them, suggest pilot studies based on *planned variation*. These studies, which could last just a few weeks, would introduce competing variations in the program at different sites. To help the planners eventually choose among them, you would check their ease of installation, their relative effect on student achievement, and staff and student satisfaction.

Example. The curriculum office of a middle-sized school district had purchased an individualized math concepts program for the primary grades. The program materials for teaching sets, counting, numeration, and place value consisted of worksheets and workbooks and sets of blocks and cards. Curriculum developers familiar with the literature in early childhood education were concerned about the adequacy of the "manipulatives" for conveying important basic math concepts. They wondered, as well, whether the materials would maintain the interest of young children. To find out whether *supplementary* materials should be used, the Director of Curriculum set up a pilot test. She purchased some Montessori counting beads and cuisenaire rods from a commercial distributor and contacted a group of interested teachers to write supplementary lessons for using the beads and rods.

When the program began in September, most of the district's schools used the new program without supplementary materials. Randomly selected schools were assigned to receive the teacher-made lessons based on commercial manipulatives. An in-service workshop was held at the end of the summer to familiarize teachers in the pilot schools with the commercial materials and locally made lessons.

The Director of Curriculum periodically monitored the entire new program, administering a math-concepts test to representative classrooms three times during the first semester. When these tests were administered, she took special care to include in the sample the classrooms using the teacher made lessons. She was therefore able to use the classes without supplementary materials as a control group against which to measure student achievement. Since development of mathematical concepts is difficult to measure in young children, she also planned to monitor teacher estimates of the suitability, ease of installment, and apparent effectiveness of the various program versions.

Planned variation studies for a program under development from scratch might emphasize the relative effectiveness of different materials and activities. Where a previously designed program is being adapted to a new locale, planned variation studies will more likely look at variations in staffing and program management.

If there is enough time, suggest a balanced set of data collection activities, including a few important pilot studies, continuous monitoring of program implementation, and periodic checks on achievement and attitudes. The precise details of these plans can be worked out under Agenda D. If possible, plan at least one service to the program that requires your frequent presence at program sites and staff meetings. This will help you stay abreast of what is happening and maintain rapport with the staff.

Arrive at a contract

Once you and your clients have reached an agreement about your role and activities, write it down. This tentative scope of work statement should include:

- A description of the evaluation questions you will address
- The data collection you have planned, including sources, sites, and instruments
- A timeline for these activities, such as the one in Table 2, page 28
- A schedule of reports and meetings, including tentative agendas where possible

Be certain to stress the *tentative* nature of this outline, allowing for changes in the program and in the needs of the staff. Also, remember *you* will be responsible for all evaluation activities contracted. Exercise your option to accept or reject assignments.

The linking agent role in formative evaluation

If you have expertise in or access to information about the subject areas the program addresses or if you know about programs of its type in operation elsewhere, you might like to append to your formative role an additional title, much in vogue—*Linking Agent*. A linking agent *connects* important accumulated information and resources with interested parties, in this case, the planners and staff of the program you are evaluating. The linking agent is a one-person information retrieval system. Her sources are libraries, journals, books, technical reports, and experts and service agencies of all kinds.

Different linking services will be relevant to different programs. For example, you might locate and describe for the staff sets of recently developed curriculum materials related to a locally developed program. If you were evaluating a special education program, you might find and make use of a regional resource center offering consultation and diagnostic help with special education students. The role of linking agent will simply broaden the range of program improvement information you collect. Be careful, however, that linking does not interfere with your primary job—to monitor and describe the program at hand.

Agenda B: Prepare a Program Statement

In Agenda A, you committed *yourself* to evaluation activities. In this agenda, the program's planners and staff commit themselves to a working description of their program. The final product of Agenda B should be a written list of

Number of personnel
work hours consumed

TABLE 2
A Summary of the
Formative Evaluator's Responsibilities

Tasks/Activities	Time in Months 19XX J J A S O N D	19YY J F M A M	Completion Date	Reports and Deliverables	Program Evaluator	Program Director	Teaching Staff	Principals	Teacher Aides	Clerical Staff
Review/revision of program plan	⊢─┤		July 31	Revised written plan	37	8	–	6	–	16
Discussion about method of formative feedback alternatives	⊢┤		Sept 15	None	16	7	24	6	–	–
Planning of implementation-monitoring activities	⊢┤		Sept 30	List of instruments; Schedules of classroom visits	60	10	24	–	–	2
Construction of implementation instruments	⊢─┤		Oct 10	Completed instruments	60	5	12	–	–	16
Planning of unit tests	⊢─┤		Oct 10	List and schedule of achievement tests	30	5	–	–	–	2
First meeting with staff	│		Nov 1	None	9	15	24	2	20	–
First meeting with district administration	│		Nov 8	First interim report	22	20	–	–	–	30
				TOTAL PERSON HOURS						

program objectives, and a *rationale* that describes the relationship between these objectives and the activities that are supposed to produce them. The program statement should reflect the current consensus about what comprises the program arrived at with the understanding that the program's character may alter over time. Although the scope of activities in Agenda B is relatively restricted, you will find that the ease of the task will depend heavily on your interpersonal skills.

Writing a preliminary program statement—even if only in outline form—is useful because it demands careful thought by the program's staff and planners about what they intend the program to look like and do. This thinking alone can lead to program improvements. Most successful programs are built upon a structured plan that has been clearly thought out and that describes as precisely as possible the program's activities, materials, and administrative arrangements. A clear program statement encourages program success for several reasons. For one thing, everybody involved knows where such a program is headed and what its critical characteristics ought to be. Everybody is working from the same plan. If program variations are taking place, then the staff and planners are likely to be aware of this. The evaluator can document such differences and, where possible, assess their merits. Fear of disputes among staff members, advisory committees, and teachers should not dissuade you from attempting to clarify program procedures and goals. Disagreements during the planning of a program are by and large healthy, especially when a program is in its *formative* stage, and the staff should be willing to adopt a "wait and see" attitude. Not all differences of opinion may be resolved, but the pooling of staff intelligence through discussion should be preferred to leaving each teacher to make his own guesses about what will work best.

Make sure that goals are well stated

There are three basic sources of information for Agenda B:

- The program plan, proposal, and other official documents
- Structured interviews and informal dialogues with program staff
- Naturalistic observation-based intuitions about program emphases

As has been mentioned, it is possible that you will arrive on the scene and find that the program has been too vaguely planned. Formative evaluation presumes the legitimacy of evaluating programs whose content and processes are still developing. Frequently the staff will be unable to tell you exactly what the program should look like, and objectives may be too general to serve as a basis for monitoring pupil progress. Although you should get a glimpse of how the program will function from documents such as the program's proposal, or the program plan, often these consist of exhaustive lists of documented *needs* that the program should meet, a page or two on objectives, and a description of the program's staffing and budget. A description of what people taking part in the program do or have done to them is not to be found.

Official documents represent *formal* statements of program intentions. These may be outdated, incomplete, erroneous, or unrealistic. Written descriptions of categorically funded programs such as ESEA Title I are particularly misleading; their objectives often reflect only politically minded rhetoric. Canned programs, or sets of published program materials, are another source of official objectives. But be careful here as well. While adoption of a particular program may reflect a philosophy shared between program staff and the developer of the materials, it is also possible that the staff running this particular program consciously or unconsciously possesses a different set of goals or that the program will only use certain components of the purchased materials.

Because of the problems associated with goals listed in official documents, you are responsible for obtaining goal information from discussions which probe the motives of the program staff and from observations of the program. Simply *asking* staff members their perceptions of program objectives will often elicit a recitation of documented goals, cliches, or socially desirable answers. Asking staff for *scenarios* of what you might see or expect to see at program sites is sometimes more productive. These scenarios can be followed by questions about the particular learning that is expected to result from the activities described. You may also find it easy to elicit statements from staff members about which aspects of the program are free to vary and which are not; this information too can shed light on the program's aims and rationale.

Record the program's rationale

Careful examination of the *rationale* underlying the program goes hand in hand with efforts to base the program on a clear and consistent plan. The rationale on which any program is based, sometimes called a process model, is simply a statement of *why* this program—a particular set of implemented materials, activities, and administrative arrangements—is expected to produce the desired outcomes. Sometimes the relationship between methods and goals is transparent; but other times, particularly with innovative programs, the credibility of the program requires that the staff explain and justify program methods and materials.

Example. A team of teachers from four high schools in a large metropolitan area planned a work-study program. The purpose of the program was to teach *careering savvy.* The teachers defined this as "knowledge about what it takes to be successful in one's chosen field of endeavor." The district assigned a consultant to the project, Anna Smith, whose job it was to help teachers iron out administrative details involved with coordinating student placement. Ms. Smith had also been told to serve in whatever formative evaluation capacity seemed necessary.

Having discovered that the teachers did not write a proposal for the program, she asked that they meet with her so that she could write a short document describing the program's major goals and outlining at least the skeleton of the program. At this meeting the teachers described the basic program. Students would choose from among a set of community-wide jobs made available at minimum pay by various professional and business firms. The students would work as office clerks, sales persons, receptionists; they might be called on to make deliveries and do odd jobs.

Instantly Ms. Smith saw that the program was without a clear rationale. "What makes you think," she asked, "that students will gain an understanding of the important skills involved in carrying on a career as a result of their taking on menial jobs?"

The staff had to admit that the program as planned did not guarantee that students would learn about the duties of people in different careers or about prerequisite skills for success. Together with Ms. Smith they restructured the program as follows:

● They added an observation-and-conversation component to ensure that sponsoring professionals and business people would commit some time to describing their personal career histories and would allow the students to observe the course of their work day.

● Students would be required to keep journals and read about the career of interest.

The formative evaluator should see to it that the program rationale is suited to the conditions under which the program will be carried out. A mismatch may arise, for example, from staff insensitivity to time needed for the program to produce its effects. This could be reflected in too many objectives or objectives that are too ambitious for a project of moderate duration.

Lack of a clear program statement does not necessarily mean that goals, a program rationale, and plans for activities do not exist.[3] Producing a program statement is most often a matter of helping the staff and planners to coordinate their intentions and shape their ideas.

Production of the *written* statement provides a good opportunity for planners to describe concretely the program they envision. Because you have the job of *writing* an official statement *for the staff,* you will be able to ask difficult questions without implying any criticism. In describing goals and activities, and especially in exploring the logic of the connection between them, the program staff may encounter contradictions, uncertainties, and conflicts that you will have to handle with tact, patience, and persistence. Their sense of ease with you in your evaluator role will be reflected in the degree of candor with which they participate in these discussions. Interviews with program staff and first-hand observations might need to replace group discussions as your primary source of information if staff members find it too hard to articulate goals, strategies, and rationale in group settings.

Work on Agenda B can proceed concurrently with work on Agenda A. Since you will be meeting with the program staff to reach agreement on your relative roles, you might also use these meetings to clarify program goals, describe implementation plans, and work out the rationale.

The staff, finally, should keep in mind that the program statement you produce is a *working document.* You, and they, will update it periodically, perhaps at the end of each reporting interval you have agreed upon. In the meantime, the existing document will be useful to people interested in the program. Besides guiding both the program as implemented and the evaluation, it can serve as the basis of reports and public relations documents.

---

3. If, in fact, there is a total lack of consensus concerning what the program is about, you may find it necessary to do a retrospective needs assessment with the staff. Needs assessments result in lists of prioritized goals, determined by polling the wants of the educational constituency and determining how well these wants are being filled by the current program. Needs assessment is discussed in greater detail on page 8.

Agenda C: Monitor Program Implementation and the Achievement of Program Objectives

One of the distinctive features of formative evaluation is the continuous description and monitoring of the program as it develops, including measurement of the impact it is having on the attitudes and achievement of its target groups. The first two agendas focus on tentative agreements about the program's scope, rationale, planned activities, and goals. With Agenda C, you begin to investigate the match between the paper program, filled with intentions and plans, and the program in operation. The information you gather about the program for Agenda C can be used to:

- Pinpoint areas of program strength and weakness
- Refine and revise the program statement and, possibly, your evaluation plan
- Hypothesize about cause-effect relationships between program features and outcomes
- Draw conclusions about the relative effectiveness of program components where you have been able to use good evaluation design and credible measures

Agenda C is the phase of formative evaluation with the strongest research flavor. It can involve selecting samples; developing, trying out, selecting, administering, and scoring instruments; and analyzing and interpreting data. The component books of the *Program Evaluation Kit* will be most useful for this phase of the evaluation. In addition, if you will be conducting pilot studies, or if your evaluation can use a randomized control group, then you can refer to Chapter 5—the *Step-by-Step Guide For Conducting a Small Experiment* for more precise guidance.

In carrying out Agenda C, as with the others, you and the audience share information with a view toward producing a product. In this case, the product is an analysis, sometimes summarized in an interim report, of the program's implementation and its progress toward achieving its objectives. You tell the program staff at this point about the specifics of your sampling plan and site selection, and the measures you have chosen to purchase or construct in order to study features of program implementation or to monitor the attitudes or achievement of different subgroups. You might, in addition, describe the pilot tests or case studies you have chosen to pursue.

The first task of the *program staff* during Agenda C is to respond to your data gathering plan, suggesting adjustments to focus it more closely on what they most want to know. They should also confer with you in order to ensure that your measurements will not be too intrusive on program activities or personnel. Finally, they should share with you their perceptions of the credibility of the information you propose to collect.

Once you have reported results to the staff and planners from one round of data collection, the audience's job will be, quite naturally, to carefully examine what you have said and choose a course of action.

The degree to which *your own personal opinions* should guide your data collection and reporting is, incidentally, something to be negotiated with staff and planners. You could, on the one hand, take the stance of an impartial conduit for transporting the information the staff feels it needs. At another extreme, you could be highly opinionated, calling staff attention to what you feel are the program's most critical and problematic processes and outcomes. In the former situation, your report will convey to program planners the data you collected with the postscript, "Now *you* make the decision." If you plan to express opinions, then your reports will likely advocate a course of action, and the data collected will be planned with an eye toward providing evidence to support your case.

Formative data collection plans

Ideally it would be nice if the formative evaluator could remain on-site with the program for extended periods of time, in the style of the participant-observer. Realistically, however, it is likely that budget, time, and possibly the geographical distribution of program sites, will make such vigilance impossible. You will have to rely on sampling, good rapport with the staff, and a well-designed measurement plan to give you an accurate picture of the program and its effects.

Your major source of first-hand information about the program will be your own informal observations and conversations with staff members while on site. Their descriptions of the program and explanations of what you see occurring should give you a good idea of how to design more formal data gathering instruments. Informal observations should also show where the program is going well and where it is failing, where a program component has been efficiently carried out, where it is partially implemented, and where it is not taking place.

In order to ensure that your informal impressions are representative and accurate, more formal data gathering will be necessary. For the purpose of formative evaluation, three approaches to collecting data about the program seem most useful:

- Periodic program monitoring
- Unit testing
- Pilot and feasibility studies

Your choice will be primarily determined by what you want to know.

Periodic program monitoring. The formative evaluator who wishes to check for proper program implementation throughout the evaluation selects a target set of characteristics which he then monitors periodically and at various sites. He also may select or construct achievement tests and attitude instruments to assess at these times the attainment of objectives of interest to the staff. The sites supplying formative information and the times at which this information is collected are often based on a sampling plan to ensure that the measurements made at intervals reflect the program as a whole.

Example. Leonard Pierson, assistant to a district's Director of Research and Evaluation, was asked to serve as formative evaluator during the first year of a parent education program. The purpose of the program was to train parents of preschool children to tutor them at home in skills related to reading readiness: classification of objects, concept formation, basic math and counting, conversation and vocabulary. Federal funds had been provided for the training and to purchase home workbooks which were supplied free of charge. These workbooks sequenced and structured the home tutoring. They contained lessons, suggestions for enrichment activities, and short periodic assessment tests. The parent training centers were set up at six community agencies and schools throughout the district. Local teachers conducted evening classes to teach parents to use the workbooks daily with their children at home.

When the project director contacted Mr. Pierson, he was simply asked to give whatever formative evaluation help he could. Mr. Pierson, free to define his own role, decided to focus on four questions:

- Most importantly, do students learn the skills that are emphasized by the workbook?
- To what extent do parents actually work with their child daily?
- Do parents use techniques taught them in the training course, or do they develop their own?
- Are their own techniques more or less effective than those they have been trained to use?

In order to help answer these questions, Mr. Pierson designed two instruments and a monitoring system for administering them periodically:

- A general achievement test consisting of items sampled from the progress tests in the workbooks. The test will be administered every six weeks to a sample of participants' children. Presumably scores on this test should increase over time. A control group will also take the test every six weeks to account for learning due to sheer maturation.
- An observation instrument to be completed by the community member who visits the home to give the six weekly achievement tests. The instrument records the amount of progress made in the workbooks since the last visit, the nature of the teaching methods used by the parent, and the apparent appropriateness of the current lesson to the student's skills—that is, whether it seems to be too difficult. Observers will be trained to be particularly alert to changes in teaching style, recording both deviations and innovations.

The details of a periodic monitoring plan are usually agreed to by the evaluator and planners at the beginning of the formative evaluation and then vary little throughout the evaluator's collaboration with the program. The periodic program monitor submits interim reports at the conclusion of each data gathering phase. Like Table 3, these often focus on whether the program is on schedule.

A formative evaluator can use Table 3 to report to the program director and the staff at each location the results of monthly site visits. Each interim report could include an updated table accompanied by explanations of why ratings of "U," unsatisfactory implementation, have been assigned. The occasion at which measurements are made are determined by the passage of standard intervals—a month, a semester—or by logical transition periods in the program—such as the dates of completion of critical units. The evaluator might check time and again at the same sites or with the same people, or he could select a different representative sample to provide data at each occasion.

TABLE 3
Project Monitoring--Activities[4]

Objective 6: By February 29, 19YY, each participating school will implement, evaluate results, and make revisions in a program for the establishment of a positive climate for learning.   Winona School District
Wiley School

Activities for this objective	Sep	Oct	Nov	Dec	Jan	Feb	Mar	Apr
6.1 Identify staff to participate		I	C					
6.2 Selected staff members review ideas, goals, and objectives		I	P	P	C			
6.3 Identify student needs	U	I	P	C				
6.4 Identify parent needs	U	I	P	C				
6.5 Identify staff needs	U	I	P	C				
6.6 Evaluate data collected in 6.3 – 6.5						I	U	C
6.7 Identify and prioritize specific outcome goals and objectives			I	U	P	P	C	
6.8 Identify existing policies, procedures, and laws dealing with positive school climate	U	I	P	P	C			

Evaluator's Periodic Progress Rating:
I = Activity Initiated   P = Satisfactory Progress
C = Activity Completed   U = Unsatisfactory Progress

Where the same measures are used repeatedly at the same sites, periodic monitoring resembles a time-series research design. This permits the evaluator to form a defensible interpretation of the program's role in bringing about the changes recorded in achievement and attitudes. Using a control group whose progress is also monitored further helps the evaluator to estimate how program students would be performing if there were no program.

Unit testing. An evaluator can focus on individual units of instruction or segments of the program that the staff has identified as particularly critical or problematic. In this case, monitoring of implementation will require *in-depth* scrutiny of the *particular* program component under study. Because the evaluator's task is to determine the value of specific program components, the implementation of these components will need to be described in as detailed a way as possible. Achievement tests, attitude instruments, and other outcome measures will have to be sensitive to the objectives that units of interest address. This could make it necessary for the evaluator to tailor-make a test, since general attitude and achievement tests will be unlikely to address the particular outcomes of interest. In some cases, the curriculum's own end-of-unit tests can be administered. If you use curriculum embedded tests, however, be careful that they are not so filled with the program's own format and content idiosyncracies that they sacrifice generalizability to other contexts or make the control group's performance look misleadingly bad. The occasions on which measurements are made for unit testing are determined by when important units occur during the course of the program. Sampling of *sites* and *participants* should be done where it is inadvisable or impractical to measure all students, but representative subgroups of students or classrooms can be measured or observed.

---

4. This table has been adapted from a formative monitoring procedure developed by Marvin C. Alkin.

Reports about the effectiveness of these critical program events should be delivered in time for modifications to be made in similar units, or in the same units in preparation for the next time a group of program participants encounters them.

If the teaching of units can be staggered at different sites so that not all students are being taught the same unit at the same time, then the results of unit tests can be used to make decisions about the best way to teach that unit at sites where it has not yet been introduced. Using a *control* *group* for unit testing gives quicker information about the relative effectiveness of different ways to implement the unit in question—more than one version can be tried out at the same time and their relative effectiveness assessed. Unit testing with a control group amounts to the same thing as a pilot or feasibility study.

Pilot and feasibility studies. These are usually undertaken because members of the program staff or its planners have in mind a particular set of issues that they need to settle or a hard decision to make. Pilot and feasibility studies are carefully conducted and usually experimental efforts to judge the relative quality of two or more ways to implement a particular program component. Pilot studies could be undertaken, for instance, to determine the most effective order in which to present information in a science discovery lab or the most beneficial time to switch students in a bilingual program to an all-English reading group. These studies require that different competing versions of a program component be installed at various sites. The evaluator first checks the degree to which each site carried out the program variation it was assigned; then, after giving the variation time to produce the results, he tests for their relative effectiveness. Like unit testing, feasibility studies demand measurement instruments that are sensitive to the outcomes that the program versions aim to produce. They usually demand random sampling since they use statistical tests to look for significant differences in the performance of groups experiencing different program variations. Pilot tests generally take place either before the program has begun, or *ad hoc* throughout the course of the evaluation whenever controversy or lack of information creates a need to try variations of the program.

Example 1. Dr. Schwartz, the university professor working as a formative evaluator for educational television station KDKC, overheard a conversation one day between two writers working on an episode for a series on cultural awareness. "*Poverty and Potatoes* is a silly name for an episode on Ireland," one writer was saying. "Well, maybe you can do better; but I say we need catchy titles—things that will make the kids want to watch," the other writer retorted. Dr. Schwartz offered to help the writers find such a title. He suggested that for each episode of the program, they write four or five possible titles. He would then construct and administer a questionnaire for students in order to find out from the target audience which title would most entice them to watch a television program.

Example 2. The Stone City school board voted in January to dismantle special classrooms for the educationally handicapped and return EH students to the regular classroom beginning in September. EH students would spend most of their time in the regular classroom, but would be "pulled out" each day to work with a special education teacher at a resource room in the school. The change would mean not only shifting students and altering the job roles of special education teachers; it would demand establishing resource rooms in schools which did not previously have them.

Faced with this large change of delivery of special education services, the district Director of Special Education suggested that some pilot work done during the present school year could prevent mistakes when mainstreaming took effect in the whole district in September. With board approval, she decided to phase mainstreaming into eight of the district's schools during the spring:

Phase I. Two schools which already had resource rooms would move EH students into the regular classrooms in March. The Director of Special Education would carefully observe and informally interview teachers, students, and special education teachers at these two schools to identify major problems involved in the transition. She would then work out an instructional package for teachers and parents that could be used to alleviate some of the problems and misunderstandings that could coincide with the organizational change.

Phase II. In April, three additional schools would be mainstreamed, using the training and counseling package developed during the first phase. Again, the effectiveness and smoothness of the transition to mainstreaming would be assessed, based on observations and interviews with regular teachers, special education teachers, students, and parents. The April sample would include one school which had not used resource rooms in the past. This would give the director a notion of the effect of mainstreaming in situations where it represents an even larger departure from regular practice. The training package would be revised based on feedback from teachers and parents with whom it was used.

Phase III. In May, three schools which had not previously had resource rooms would be converted to mainstreaming. The experience of the first two phases hopefully would make this transition a smooth one.

The Director of Special Education, having experienced several months of work in mainstreaming, could spend the summer preparing materials for parents and training teachers to anticipate September's reorganization.

Pilot and feasibility tests usually occur only when the evaluator offers to do them. Planners do not usually ask to have this sort of service performed for them. A feasibility study need not, as well, be based on achievement outcomes. A common question it might address is "Will people like Version X better than Version Y?"

Whatever plan you use for monitoring the program's effects, your efforts will allow the staff to make data-based judgments about whether program procedures are having an effect on participants. Besides the outcomes that planners hope to produce, you will need to look vigilantly for *unintended* outcomes—side-effects that can be ascribed to the program but which have not been mentioned by planners or listed in official documents. Although side-effects are generally thought of as negative, they could as easily be beneficial. You might discover, for example, potentially effective practices spontaneously implemented at a few sites that are worth exporting to others. Negative unintended effects are important to discover if the program is to be improved. They highlight areas that require added attention, modification, or even discarding.

Remember that when the data you collect suggest revisions in the program, you will have to amend the program

TABLE 4
Contrasts Between Reports for Formative and Summative Evaluation

	Formative Report	Summative Report
Purpose	Shows the results of monitoring the program's implementation or of pilot tests conducted during the course of the program's installation. Intended to help change something going on in the program that is not working as well as it might, or to expand a practice or special activity that shows promise.	*Documents* the program's implementation either at the *conclusion* of a developmental period or when it has had sufficient time to undergo refinement and work smoothly. Intended to put the program on record, to describe it as a finished work.
Tone	Informal	Usually formal
Form	Can be written or audiovisual; can be delivered to a group as a speech, or take the form of informal conversations with the project director or staff, etc.	Nearly always written, although some formal, verbal presentation might be made to supplement or explain the report's conclusions.
Length	Variable	Variable, but sufficiently *condensed* or *summarized* that it can be used to help planners or decision makers who have little time to spend reading at a highly detailed level.
Level of specificity	*High,* focusing on particular activities or materials used by particular people, or on what happened with particular students and at a certain place or point in time.	Usually more *moderate,* attempting to document general program characteristics common to many sites so that summary statements and general, overall decisions can be made.

statement as well. Program staff should take part in making these revisions, and consensus should be reached before any changes are recorded in the program's official description. New program statements may also suggest revisions or additions to your contracted evaluation activities.

Agenda D: Report and Confer With Planners and Staff

The reporting mode for formative evaluation varies with the situation. As is shown in Table 4, formative reports almost never look like the more technical ones submitted by summative evaluators. Most formative reporting takes place in conversations or discussions that the evaluator has with individuals or groups of program personnel. The form of *your* report will depend on:

- The reporting style that is most comfortable to you and the staff with whom you are working
- The extent to which *official* records are required
- Whether you will disseminate results only among program sites, or to interested outsiders and the general community as well
- How soon the information must reach its audience in order to be useful
- How the information will be used

Whether reports are oral or written is up to you. If additional planning or program modification will be based

on the reports you give, then it is best to *discuss* program effects with the staff, perhaps at a problem solving meeting, so that remedies for problems can be debated and decisions made.

A *written* report provides a documentation of activities and findings to which the audience can continually refer and that can be used in program planning and revision. Written reports, however, take time to draft, polish, discuss, and revise. This is time that might be better spent collecting information and working on program development with the staff. In many cases, the best way to leave a written trace of the results of your formative findings will be to periodically revise the program statement you produced as part of Agenda B.

Face-to-face meetings provide the staff and planners with a forum for discussion, clarification, and detailed elaboration of the evaluation's findings as well as the opportunity for making suggestions about upcoming evaluation activities. During conversational reports, you will be able to make requests for assistance in solving logistical problems or collecting data. Staff members might also want to express their problems or suggest new information needs.

A schedule for *interim reports* should be part of the evaluation contract. The program staff should indicate when or how frequently they wish to review the results of each evaluation activity. Interim reports on the progress of program development should contain results of completed evaluation components, a reiteration of tasks yet to be accomplished, and a full description and rationale for any changes in your responsibilities that may have to be negotiated.

Formative evaluation reports can include feedback of different sorts. At minimum, such a report will simply describe what the formative evaluator saw taking place—what the program looked like and what achievement or attitudes appeared to be the result. Depending upon his presumed expertise in such matters, the formative evaluator may also make suggestions about changes, point to places where the program is in particular need, and offer services to help remedy these problems. Your contributions along these lines will depend on your expertise and the contract you have worked out with the planners and staff.

If your evaluation service has focussed on pilot or feasibility studies, then your report will follow a more standard outline, although you may supplement the discussion of the results with recommendations for adaptation, adoption, or rejection of certain program components and perhaps outline further studies that are needed.

The tentative nature of instructional components in the formative stages of a program should be a recurring theme in your conversations with and reports to the staff. You will find that once teachers and staff are comfortable with program procedures, they will want to avoid making further changes in the program. The formative evaluator will have to make a conscious effort to keep the staff interested in looking at program materials and procedures with a view toward making them *yet more* appropriate, effective, and appealing for the students. Although evaluators will have the responsibility of overseeing the collection of informa-

tion to support decisions about program revisions, the suggestions and active involvement of teachers in this decision-making process is crucial. Everyone on the program staff should understand why the formative evaluation is occurring and should be encouraged to take part.

For Further Reading

Alkin, M. C., Daillak, R., & White, P. *Using evaluations: does evaluation make a difference?* Sage Library of Social Research. Beverly Hills, CA: Sage Pubns., 1979.

Baker, E. L., & Saloutos, A. G. *Evaluating instructional programs.* Los Angeles, CA: Center for the Study of Evaluation, 1974.

Havelock, R. G. *Planning for innovation through dissemination and utilization of knowledge.* Center for Research on Utilization of Scientific Knowledge, Institute for Social Research, University of Michigan, January, 1971.

Lichfield, N., Kettle, P., & Whitbread, M. *Evaluation in the planning process.* Oxford: Pergamon Press, 1975.

Nash, N., & Culbertson, J. (Eds). *Linking processes in educational improvement.* Columbus, OH: University Council for Educational Administration, 1977.

Patton, M. Q. *Utilization-focused evaluation.* Beverly Hills, CA: Sage Publications, 1978.

Chapter 2 listed some of the myriad jobs of the formative evaluator. This role, it was mentioned, is most easily described in terms of the goal the formative evaluator has in mind—to collect and share with planners and staff information that will lead to improvement in a developing program. The diversified nature of formative evaluation might make providing a step-by-step guide seem a little silly or arbitrary. In truth, there is no step-by-step way to perform the tasks involved with the role.

Enough activities are common among formative evaluations, however, to permit a general outline of what needs to be accomplished. Chapter 2 described four *agendas*—goals with accompanying tasks—to which any formative evaluator must attend to some degree. These agendas are:

- *Agenda A. Set the Boundaries of the Evaluation;* that is, negotiate the scope of the data gathering activities in which you will engage, the aspects of the program on which you will concentrate, and the responsibilities of your audience to cooperate in the collection of data and to use the information you supply.

- *Agenda B. Prepare a Program Statement,* a clear description of program goals accompanied by a *rationale* describing why program activities are thought to lead to these goals.

- *Agenda C. Monitor Program Implementation and the Achievement of Program Objectives.* This includes periodic measurement to inform the staff about whether the program is on schedule and operating as planned and to check whether progress is being made in achieving desired outcomes.

- *Agenda D. Report and Confer With Planners and Staff* about changes to be made in the program and about additional formative activities.

Included in this chapter are step-by-step guides for *each* of these agendas. Each guide lists the major events that might take place in completing the agenda. You can look at the step-by-step guide as a reminder of critical decisions that need to be made while working at a particular stage of a formative evaluation. The step-by-step guides should prompt you to be thoughtful in planning what you do, collecting information and talking with the program staff. Each guide can serve as a *checklist* to help you keep track

of what you have completed in the process of serving the program and to give you ideas about where to go and what to do next.

As Chapter 2 mentioned, many of the tasks falling within the scope of the different agendas will actually occur simultaneously or in an order other than that described by the step-by-step guide. In general, however, there will be some logical order to how your evaluation unfolds. You will do most of Agenda A, for instance, before you begin Agenda C; and the tasks in Agenda D, since they involve reporting and sharing information, will likely occur toward the end of information gathering cycles. Consider the step-by-step guides, then, a loose map of the activities formative evaluators might find themselves performing. You will almost certainly have to attend in some way to many of the tasks listed in each agenda. Use the step-by-step guides as you like.

An important thing to notice about the agendas is that they demand equal sharing of information between the formative evaluator and her audience. Each agenda produces a product. The product of the first agenda, during which roles are defined and the evaluation gets started, is a *contract,* or at least an outline, of the mutual responsibilities of the evaluator and the planners and staff. The product of the second agenda is a clarified *program statement,* complete with goals, a description of program implementation, and a rationale. Agenda C, which includes *program monitoring,* probably the evaluator's major responsibility, produces analyzed and summarized information about the quality of program implementation, attitudes, and achievement. Reporting of this information is so important to formative evaluation that it is relegated its own agenda—Agenda D.

If you are working as a formative evaluator for the first time in the setting, your best guidance might come from a conversation with someone who has evaluated the program before or who has served as formative evaluator in a similar setting. If formative evaluation presents a change in the evaluation role to which you are accustomed, then seek out someone who has done it before. Nothing beats advice from long experience.

Whenever possible, the step-by-step guides use checklists and worksheets to help you keep track of what you have decided and found out. Actually, the worksheets might be better called "guidesheets," since you will have to copy many of them onto your own paper rather than use the one in the book. Space simply does not permit the book to provide places to list large quantities of data.

As you use the guides, you will come upon references marked by the symbol ◢◣. These direct you to read sections of various *How To* books contained in the *Program Evaluation Kit*. At these junctures in the evaluation, it will be necessary for you to review a concept or follow a procedure outlined in one of these seven resource books:

- *How To Deal With Goals and Objectives*
- *How To Design a Program Evaluation*
- *How To Measure Program Implementation*
- *How To Measure Attitudes*
- *How To Measure Achievement*
- *How To Calculate Statistics*
- *How To Present an Evaluation Report.*

To give you an overview of the formative evaluation tasks included in the guides, a flow chart showing the steps required to complete each agenda appears at the beginning of each step-by-step guide.

Set the Boundaries
of the Evaluation

Instructions
===

Agenda A encompasses the evaluation planning
period--from the time you accept the job of formative evaluator until you begin to actually carry
out the assignments dictated by the role. Much
of Agenda A amounts to gaining an understanding of
the program and outlining the services you can
perform, then negotiating them with the members
of the staff who will use formative information.

Agenda A's five steps and twelve substeps are
outlined by this flowchart:

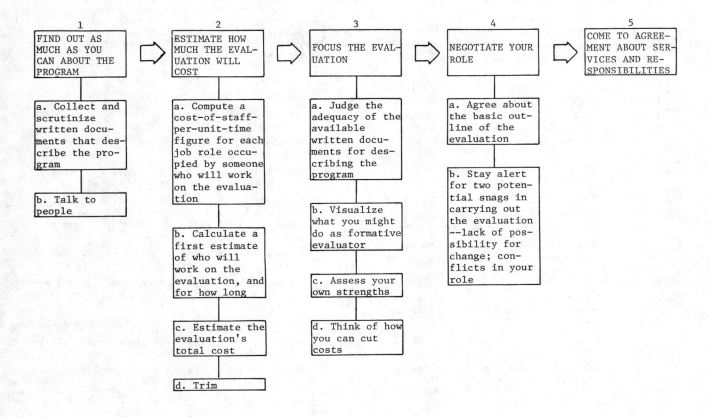

1	2	3	4	5
FIND OUT AS MUCH AS YOU CAN ABOUT THE PROGRAM	ESTIMATE HOW MUCH THE EVAL-UATION WILL COST	FOCUS THE EVAL-UATION	NEGOTIATE YOUR ROLE	COME TO AGREE-MENT ABOUT SER-VICES AND RE-SPONSIBILITIES
a. Collect and scrutinize written docu-ments that des-cribe the pro-gram	a. Compute a cost-of-staff-per-unit-time figure for each job role occu-pied by someone who will work on the evalua-tion	a. Judge the adequacy of the available written docu-ments for des-cribing the program	a. Agree about the basic out-line of the evaluation	
b. Talk to people	b. Calculate a first estimate of who will work on the evaluation, and for how long	b. Visualize what you might do as formative evaluator	b. Stay alert for two poten-tial snags in carrying out the evaluation --lack of pos-sibility for change; con-flicts in your role	
	c. Estimate the evaluation's total cost	c. Assess your own strengths		
	d. Trim	d. Think of how you can cut costs		

Find out as much as you can about the program

Instructions

a. Collect and scrutinize written documents that describe the program

CHECK ✓ ☐   Check whether you can obtain copies of the following:

☐ A program proposal written for the funding agency

☐ The request for proposals (RFP) written by the sponsor or funding agency to which this program's proposal was a response

☐ Results of a needs assessment* whose findings the program is intended to address

☐ Written state or district guidelines about program processes and goals, to which this program must conform

☐ The program's budget, particularly the part that mentions the evaluation

☐ A description of, or an organizational chart depicting, the administrative and staff roles played by various people in the program

☐ Curriculum guides for the materials which have been purchased for the program

☐ Past evaluations of this or similar programs

☐ Lists of goals and objectives which the staff or planners feel describe the program's aims

☐ Tests or surveys which the program planners feel may be used to measure the effects of the program, such as a district-wide year end assessment instrument

☐ Memos, meeting minutes, newspaper articles-- descriptions made by the staff or the planners of the program

---

*A needs assessment is an announcement of educational needs, expressed in terms of school curriculum and policies, by representatives of the school or district constituency.

☐ Descriptions of the program's history, or of the social context which it has been designed to fit

☐ Articles in the education and evaluation literature that describe the effects of programs such as the one in question, its curricular materials, or its various subcomponents

☐ Other _____

Once you have discovered which materials are available, seek them out and copy them if possible. Make notes in the margins. Write down or dictate onto tape comments about your general impression of the program, its context, and staff.

CHECK ✓ ☐   Find out, if possible, about these components of the program:

☐ The program's major general goals

☐ Specifically stated objectives

☐ The philosophy or point of view of the program planners

☐ Examples of similar programs that planners intend to emulate

☐ Writers in the field of education whose point of view the program is intended to mirror

☐ The needs of the community or constituency which the program is intended to meet--whether these have been explicitly stated or seem to implicitly underly the program

☐ Program implementation directives and requirements

☐ The amount of variation from site to site, or even student to student, that will be tolerated by the program

☐ The number and distribution of sites involved

☐ Canned or prepublished curricula which will be used for the program

☐ Curriculum materials which will be constructed in-house

☐ Plans for in-service training

☐ Plans for curriculum development

☐ Plans which have been developed describing how the program will look in operation--times of day, scripts for lessons, etc.

☐ Administrative, decision-making, and teaching roles to be played by various people

☐ Student evaluation plans

☐ Teacher evaluation plans

☐ Program evaluation plans

☐ Staff responsibilities

☐ Timelines and deadlines for accomplishing particular implementation goals or reaching certain levels of student achievement

b. Talk to people

Once you have arrived at a set of initial impressions, check these--and your germinating evaluation plans--by seeking out people who can give you two kinds of information:

• Advice about how to go about collecting formative information for a program of this sort

• Answers to your questions about what the program is supposed to be and do--including <u>which</u> and <u>how much</u> modification can occur based on your findings

By all means, find the people with whom you will

 have most contact and who will be in a position to use the information you collect. These people might be:

☐ The project director(s)

☐ Evaluators and consultants who have worked with the program or its staff in the past

_____

_____

☐ Evaluators who have worked with this type of program in the past

_____

_____

☐ Teachers, particularly those who seem to have most influence

_____

_____

☐ Program planners and designers

☐ Curriculum consultants to the project

☐ Members of advisory committees

_____

_____

☐ School or district personnel not directly connected with the project, but whose cooperation will help you carry out the evaluation more efficiently or quickly

☐ Influential parents

_____

_____

☐ Influential or particularly helpful students

_____

_____

☐ The people who wrote the proposal

_____

_____

Try to think of other people involved with the program whose opinions and decisions will influence the success of the evaluation and the extent to which the information you collect will be useful and used. Make sure that you talk with each of these people, either at a group meeting or individually.

 If they are too busy to talk, send memos to key people. Describe the evaluation, what you would like them to do for you, and when.

In your meetings with these people, <u>you</u> should communicate two things:

• Who you are and why you are formatively evaluating the program

• The importance of your staying in contact with them throughout the course of the evaluation

<u>They</u>, in turn, should point out to you:

• Areas in which you have misunderstood the program's objectives or its description

• Parts of the program which will be alternatively emphasized or relatively disregarded during the term of the evaluation

• Their decision about the boundaries of the cooperation they will give you

 Keep a list of the addresses and phone numbers of the people you have contacted with notations about the best time of day to call them or the times when it is easiest for them to attend meetings.

 If possible, observe the program in operation, or programs like it. Accompanied by program planners and staff, take a field trip to look at one or two similar programs. This will help the staff react to what they see. It will give you and them a better idea of what the program is supposed to look like and how it could change.

Take careful notes of everything you see and do. Later you may find some of these valuable.

Estimate how much the evaluation will cost

Instructions

If the project intends to pay for your services, you will have to determine early the financial bounds that constrain the evaluation.

The cost of an evaluation is difficult to predict accurately. This is unfortunate, since what you will be able to promise the staff and planners will be determined by what you feel you can afford to do.

Estimate costs by getting the easy ones out of the way first. Find out <u>costs per unit</u> for each of these "fixed" expenses:

☐ Postage and shipping (bulk rate, parcel post, etc.)   _____

☐ Photocopying and printing   _____

☐ Travel and transportation   _____

☐ Long-distance phone calls   _____

☐ Test and instrument purchase   _____

☐ Consultants   _____

☐ Mechanical test or questionnaire scoring   _____

☐ Data processing   _____

These fixed costs will come "off the top" each time you sketch out the budget accompanying an alternative method for evaluating the program.

The most difficult cost to estimate is the most important one: the price of person-hours required for your services and those of the staff you assemble for the evaluation. If you are inexperienced, try to emulate other people. Ask how other evaluators estimate costs and then do likewise.

<u>Develop a rule-of-thumb that computes the cost of each type of evaluation staff member per unit time period</u>, such as "It costs $4,500 for one senior evaluator, working full time, per month." This figure should summarize all expenses of the evaluation, excluding only overhead and costs unique to a particular study--such as travel and data analysis.

The <u>staff cost per unit</u> figure should include:

The salary of a staff member for that time unit

+ His benefits

+ Office and equipment rental

+ Secretarial and support services

+ Telephones

+ Utilities

→ This equals the total routine expenses of running your office for the time unit in question, divided by the number of full-time evaluators working there.

Compute such a figure for each evaluation staff salary classification--PhD's, Masters' level staff, data gatherers, etc. Since the cost of each of these staff positions will differ, you can plan variously priced evaluations by juggling amounts of time to be spent on the evaluation by staff members in different salary brackets.

The <u>tasks</u> you promise to perform will in turn determine and be determined by the amount of time you can allot to the evaluation from different staff levels. A formative evaluation will cost more if it requires the attention of skilled evaluators, with repeated feedback to staff, and possibly pilot studies, than if it simply establishes an overall monitoring system where graduate students or teachers routinely collect data.

    To estimate the cost of your evaluation, try these steps:

a. <u>Compute a cost-of-staff-per-unit-time figure for each job role occupied by someone who will work on the evaluation</u>

Depending on the amount of backup staff support entered into the equation, this figure could be as high as twice the gross salary earned by a person in that position.

b. <u>Calculate a first estimate of who will work on the evaluation, and for how long</u>

c. Estimate the evaluation's total cost

 Refer to the proposed time span of the evaluation. Be sure to include fixed costs unique to the evaluation --travel, printing, long-distance phone calls, etc., and your indirect or overhead costs if any. Discuss this figure with the funding source, or compare it with the amount you know to be already earmarked for the evaluation.

d. Trim

 See if one or more of the following strategies will reduce your requirement for expensive personnel time, or trim some of the fixed costs:

☐ Sampling. Rather than visiting an entire population of program sites, for instance, visit a small sample of them, perhaps a third. Send observers with checklists to a slightly larger sample, and perhaps send questionnaires to the whole group of sites to corroborate the findings of the visits and observers.

☐ Employing junior staff members for some of the design, data gathering, and report writing tasks

☐ Finding volunteer help, perhaps by persuading the staff that you can supply richer and more varied information or reach more sites if you have their cooperation

☐ Purchasing measures rather than designing your own

☐ Cutting planning time by building the evaluation on procedures that you, or people whose expertise you can easily tap, have used before

☐ Consolidating instruments and the times of their administration

☐ Planning to look at different sites with different degrees of thoroughness, concentrating your efforts on those factors of greatest importance

☐ Using pencil-and-paper instruments that can be machine read and scored where possible

☐ Relying more heavily on information that will be collected by others, such as state administered tests and records that are part of the program

Focus the evaluation

Instructions
===

a. <u>Judge the adequacy of the available written documents for describing the program</u>

DECISION

Make a note of your impressions of the <u>quality</u> and specificity of the program's written description. Answer these questions in particular:

- Are the written documents <u>specific enough</u> to give you a good picture of what will happen? Do they suggest which components you will evaluate and what they will look like?

  ☐ yes   ☐ no   ☐ uncertain

  _____
  _____

- Have program planners written a clear <u>rationale</u> describing <u>why</u> the particular activities, processes, materials, and administrative arrangements in the program will lead to the goals and objectives specified for the program?

  ☐ yes   ☐ no   ☐ uncertain

  _____
  _____

- Is the program that is planned, and/or the goals and objectives toward which it aims, consistent with the philosophy or point of view on which the program is based? Do you note <u>misinterpretations</u> or conflicting interpretations anywhere?

  ☐ yes   ☐ no   ☐ uncertain

  _____
  _____

If your answers to any of these questions is <u>no</u> or <u>uncertain</u>, then you will have to include in your evaluation plans discussions with the planners and staff to persuade them to set down a clear statement of the program's goals and rationale.

b. <u>Visualize what you might do as formative evaluator</u>

DECISION

Base this exercise upon your impressions of the program:

- Which components appear to provide the key to whether it sinks or swims?_____
  _____

- Which components do the planners and staff most emphasize as being critically important?
  _____
  _____

- Which are likely to fail? Why?_____
  _____

- What might be <u>missing</u> from the program as planned that could turn out to be critical for its success?_____
  _____

- Where is the program too poorly planned to merit success?_____
  _____

- Which student outcomes will it probably be easiest to accomplish? Which will be most difficult?_____
  _____

- What effects might the program have that its planners have not anticipated?_____
  _____

<u>While conducting this exercise by yourself, do not be afraid of being hard on the program.</u> It is your job to foresee potential problems that the program's planners might overlook.

When you think about the service you can provide, you will, of course, need to consider two important things besides program characteristics and outcomes. These are the <u>budget</u> which you worked out in Step 2 and your own particular <u>strengths and talents</u>.

c. <u>Assess your own strengths</u>

 You will best benefit the program in those areas where your visualization in Step 3b matches your expertise. You should "tune" the evaluation to build on your skills as:

☐ A researcher

☐ A group process leader or organizational facilitator

☐ A subject matter "expert"--perhaps a curriculum designer

☐ A former teacher in the relevant subject areas

☐ An administrator

☐ A facilitator for problem solving

☐ A counselor or therapist

☐ A linking agent (See page 27, Chapter 2)

☐ A good listener or speaker

☐ An effective writer

☐ A synthesizer or conceptualizer

☐ A disseminator of information, or public relations promoter

☐ Other_____

d. <u>Think of how you can cut costs</u>

 Since the services you can envision providing probably exceed your budget, think of how you can cut costs. See Step 2c, page 41.

Negotiate your role

Instructions

Chapter 2 presented a general outline of the tasks
that often fall within the formative evaluator's
role. You will have to work out your own job with
your own audience. Meet again and confer with the
people whose cooperation will be necessary--those
whose decisions about the program carry most influence and who will cooperate when you gather information. You may, of course, also want to meet
with other audiences.

a. Agree about the basic outline of the evaluation

☐ Agree about the program characteristics and
outcomes that will be your major focus--regard-
less of the prominence given them in official
program descriptions. Ask the planners and
staff these questions:

• Which characteristics of the program do you
consider most important for accomplishing its
objectives? Might you have implemented it in
a different way than is currently planned?
Would you be willing to undertake a planned
variation study and try this other way?

_____

_____

• What components would you like the program to
have which are currently not planned? Might we
try some of these on a pilot basis?

_____

_____

• Are there particularly expensive, troublesome,
controversial, or difficult-to-implement parts
of the program that you might like to change or
eliminate? Could we conduct some pilot or
feasibility studies, altering these on a trial
basis at some sites?

_____

_____

• Which achievements and attitudes are of highest
priority?_____

_____

• On which achievements and attitudes do you
expect the program to have most direct and
easily observed effect?

_____

_____

• Does the program have social or political objectives that should be monitored?

_____

_____

☐ Agree about the sites and people from whom you
will collect information. Ask these questions:

• At which sites will the program be in operation?
How geographically dispersed are they?

_____

_____

• How much does the program as implemented vary
from site to site? Where can such variations
be seen?_____

_____

• Who are the important people to talk with and
observe?_____

_____

• When are the most critical times to see the
program--occasions over its duration, and also
hours during the day?

_____

_____

• At what points during the course of the program
will it be best to measure student progress,
staff attitudes, etc? Are there logical
breaking points at, say, the completion of
particular key units or semesters? Or does the
program progress steadily, or each student
individually, with no best time to measure?

_____

_____

- Would it be better to monitor the program as a whole periodically, or should the effectiveness of various program subparts be singled out for scrutinizing, or both?

_____

_____

More detailed description of sampling plans is contained in How To Measure Program Implementation, pages 60 to 64. How To Design a Program Implementation, pages 33 to 45, describes decisions you might make about when to make measurements.

☐ Agree about the part the staff will play in collecting, sharing, and providing information. Explain to the staff that its cooperation will allow you to collect richer and more credible information about the program--with a clearer message about what needs to be done. Ask:

- Can records kept during the program as a matter of course be collected or copied to provide information for the evaluation?

_____

_____

- Can record-keeping systems be established to give me needed information?

_____

_____

- Will you--teachers and staff--be able to share achievement information with me or help with its collection? Are you willing to administer periodic tests to samples of students?

_____

_____

- Will staff members be willing and able to attend brief evaluation meetings or evaluation planning sessions?_____

_____

- Will you be willing and able to take part in planned program variations or pilot tests? Will you be willing to respond to attitude surveys to determine the effectiveness of program components?_____

_____

- Based on the information I collect, will you be willing to spend time on modifying the program through new instruction, lessons, organizational or staffing patterns?_____

_____

- Are you willing to adopt a formative wait-and-see experimental attitude toward the program?

_____

_____

How To Measure Program Implementation describes ways to use records kept during the program to back up descriptions of its implementation. See pages 79 to 88.

☐ Agree about the extent to which you will be able to take a research stance toward the evaluation. Find out:

- Will it be possible to set up control groups with whom program progress can be compared?

_____

_____

- Will it be possible to establish a true control group design by randomly assigning participants to different variations of the program or to a no-program control group? Will it be possible to delay introducing the program at some sites?

_____

_____

- Can non-equivalent control groups be formed or located?_____

- Will I have a chance to make measurements prior to the program and/or often enough to set up a time series design?_____

- Will I be able to use a good design to underlie pilot tests or feasibility studies?

_____

_____

- Will I be able or required to conduct in-depth case studies at some sites?

_____

_____

Details about the use of designs in formative evaluation are discussed in How To Design a Program Evaluation. See in particular pages 14 to 19 and 46 to 51. Case studies are discussed in How To Measure Program Implementation, pages 31 and 32.

☐ Agree about the extent to which you will need to provide other services. Ask the staff and planners these questions:

- Do you need consultative help that stretches my role beyond collecting formative data? Do you want my advice about program modifications, for instance? Or help with solving personnel problems?_____

_____

- Do you want me to serve to some degree as a linking agent? Should I, for instance, conduct literature reviews, seek consultation from similar projects, or search out services or additional people or funds to help the project?

  _____

  _____

- Should I take on a public relations role? Will you want me to serve as a spokesperson for the project? To give talks or write a newsletter, for example?_____

  _____

b. **Stay alert for two potential snags in carrying out the evaluation**

- Lack of possibilities for changing the program
- Conflicts in your own responsibilities to the program and the sponsor

☐ **Look out for lack of commitment to change on the part of planners or staff.** It will be fruitless to collect data to modify the program if someone will resist modifications. Before you begin scrutinizing the program or its various components, then, you should find out where funding requirements, staff opinion, or the political surround restrict altering the program. Ask in particular the following questions:

- On <u>what</u> are you most and least willing, or constrained, to spend additional money? What materials, personnel, or facilities?

  _____

  _____

- Where would you be most agreeable to <u>cutbacks</u>? Can you, for instance, remove personnel? If particular program components were found to be ineffective, would you eliminate them? Which books, materials, and other program components would you be willing to delete?

  _____

  _____

- Would you be willing to scrap the program as it currently looks and start over?

  _____

  _____

- How much <u>administrative or staff reorganization</u> will you tolerate? Can you change people's roles? Can you add to staff, say, by bringing in volunteers? Can you move people--teachers, even students--from location to location permanently or temporarily? Can you reassign students to different programs or groups?

  _____

  _____

- How much <u>instructional and curricular change</u> will you tolerate in the program beyond its current state? Would you be willing to delete, add, or alter the program's objectives? To what extent would you be willing to change books, materials, and other program components? Are you willing to rewrite lessons?

  _____

  _____

Include additional "what if..." questions that are more specific to the program at hand.

☐ **Look out for conflicts in your own role.** If your job requires that you report about the program to its sponsor or to the community at large, staff members are likely to be reluctant to share with you doubts and conjectures about the program. Since this will hamper your effectiveness, you will do best to explain to the planners and staff the following:

- That you do not intend to write a summative report that judges and finds fault with the program. Outline the form and some of the message that the report will contain.

  and/or

- That the planners and staff will have a chance to screen reports that you submit to the sponsor.

  and/or

- That you are willing to write a final report describing only those aspects of the program chosen by the staff.

  and/or

- That you are willing to swear confidentiality about the issues and activities that the evaluation addresses.

 NOTE   If you are in a hurry, and you think that you need to purchase instruments for the evaluation, then get started on this right away. Consult Steps C3 and C4, and the relevant <u>How To</u> books, and order specimen sets as soon as possible.

Come to agreement about services and responsibilities

Instructions

An agreement outlining the duties of the formative evaluator and the program staff could conform to the following format:

This agreement, made on _____, 19__ describes a tentative outline of the formative evaluation of the _____ project, funded by _____ for the academic year _____ to _____. The evaluation will take place from _____, 19__ to _____, 19__. The formative evaluator for this project is _____ assisted by _____ and _____.

Focus of the Evaluation

The program staff has communicated its intention that the formative evaluator monitor periodically the <u>implementation</u> of the following program characteristics and components <u>across all sites</u>:

_____

_____

Implementation of the following planned or natural program variations will be monitored as well:

_____

_____

The evaluator will monitor periodically progress in the achievement of these cognitive, attitudinal, and other outcomes:

_____

_____

The evaluator, in addition, will conduct feasibility and pilot studies to answer the following questions:

_____

_____

The evaluator will provide, as well, the following services to the staff and planners:

_____

_____

Data Collection Plans

Program Monitoring and Unit Testing

Data collection for ongoing formative monitoring of implementation and progress toward objectives will take place during the following periods: from _____ to _____; from _____ to _____; and from _____ to _____. These dates were chosen because _____.

Interim reports, delivered to _____ and to _____, will be due on _____, 19__, _____, 19__, _____, 19__, and _____, 19__.

Approximately _____ program and _____ control sites for collection of <u>implementation</u> data will be chosen on a _____ (random/volunteer) basis. Of these, _____ will be studied intensively using a case study method; _____ will be examined by means of observation and interviews; and _____ will receive questionnaires or have records reviewed only. Staff members filling the following roles will be asked to cooperate:

_____

Approximately _____ program and _____ control sites will take part in each assessment of progress toward program outcomes. These will be chosen on a _____ basis.

During each assessment period listed above, the following types of instruments will be administered to students and _____:

_____

_____

Pilot and Feasibility Studies

Pilot and feasibility studies will be conducted at approximately_____ sites, chosen on a _____ basis. The purpose and probable duration of each study is outlined below:

_____
_____

Tentative completion dates for these studies are _____, 19__, _____, 19__, and _____, 19__, with reports delivered to _____ and _____ on _____, 19__, _____, 19__, and _____, 19__.

The following implementation, attitude, achievement, and other instruments will be constructed for the pilot studies:_____
_____

Staff Participation

Staff members have agreed to cooperate with and assist data collection during monitoring, unit testing, and pilot studies in the following ways:

_____
_____

Approximately _____ meetings will be needed to report and describe the evaluation's findings. These meetings, scheduled to occur a few days after submission of interim reports, will be attended by people filling the following roles:

_____

The planners and staff have agreed that decisions such as the following might result from the formative evaluation: _____
_____
_____

Budget

The evaluation as planned is anticipated to require the following expenditures:

Direct Salaries $_____

Evaluation and Assistant Benefits $_____

Other Direct Costs:
    Supplies and materials
    Travel
    Consultant services
    Equipment rental
    Communication
    Printing and duplicating
    Data processing
    Equipment purchase
    Facility rental $_____

        Total Direct Costs $_____

Indirect Costs $_____

            TOTAL COSTS $_____

Variance Clause

The staff and planners of the _____ program, and the evaluator, agree that the evaluation outlined here represents an approximation of the formative services to be delivered during the period _____, 19__ to _____, 19__.

Since both the program and the evaluation are likely to change, however, all parties agree that aspects of the evaluation can be negotiated.

The contract outlined here prescribes the evaluation's general outline only. If you plan to describe either the program or the evaluation in greater detail, then include tables such as Tables 2 and 3 in Chapter 2, pages 28 and 31.

Agenda B

Prepare a
Program Statement

Instructions

Agenda B may not be necessary if the program has been thoughtfully and specifically planned. If the program is based on adapting a canned program or curriculum to the setting, for instance, then the program is probably already accompanied by well-specified objectives and a _rationale_ describing why the program's activities are expected to achieve them.

On the other hand, if planners are building a program _de novo_, then you may have to devote considerable attention to Agenda B. Program personnel may be working from only a vague plan--one too nonspecific to underlie a successful program, let alone a useful formative evaluation.

Agenda B has three steps:

1 HOLD A MEETING TO SPECIFY THE PROGRAM'S GOALS

2 DEVELOP AND EXAMINE A PROGRAM RATIONALE

3 WRITE THE PROGRAM STATEMENT

Hold a meeting to specify the program's goals

Instructions

Meet again with the program staff to persuade them to express the outcome and implementation goals of the program in measurable terms. This will no doubt require more than rewording. It might be necessary for the staff to select whole new sets of goals and objectives which are prerequisite to accomplishing the goals they have outlined.

 Refer to How To Deal With Goals and Objectives for ideas about stating outcome goals and objectives, obtaining sets of prewritten objectives, and helping people arrive at priorities.

 Describe the goals and objectives of the program to which you think your evaluation will need to most closely attend, and ask the staff and planners to react.

 Then list program goals according to priority.

Cognitive goals:

_____

_____

Attitude goals:

_____

_____

Other goals--for instance, organizational, political, community focused:

_____

_____

 To persuade people to be more clear about what implementation of the program as planned should look like, have staff and planners complete this table:

| Crucial activities and materials in the program | A stranger who came upon the activity in operation or the materials in use would see... | | | |
	Students doing this:	Teachers doing this:	"Others" doing this:	Because

 Consult, as well, Chapter 2 of How To Measure Program Implementation. It lists questions to ask the staff to help them describe program implementation in detail.

 Then list the major characteristics of program implementation:

_____

_____

 NOTE While you are talking to people, put together, as well, preliminary plans about how you will measure goal attainment.

Say to the planners and staff members:

Now that you've stated a goal or an objective of the program, what evidence would convince you that students have met the goal or mastered the objective? What will this look like in present learning or performance? How will this look in future performance? What present performance would satisfy you that the future performance is likely to come about?

Ask them to consider as well:

• What evidence would convince you that students are not attaining the goals that you have set?

• How much of this negative evidence would it take for you to decide that the program is not accomplishing what you intended?

These are, of course, hard questions; but their
answers will determine the direction of your data
collection plans.

 If your evaluation will include a
control or comparison group to whose
performance program progress will be
compared, you will want to get some
idea of the goals and objectives, and the implementation and rationale, of the program these
students are receiving as well.

Develop and examine a program rationale

The goal of this step is to remedy the possibly detrimental effects of fuzzy thinking on the part of the people who planned the program. The program rationale is the <u>theory</u> on which the program rests. This theory should be consistent and clear enough to be understood by everyone working in the program or evaluating it.

 Consult <u>How To Measure Program Implementation</u>, pages 25 to 29, for a discussion of evaluations based on theories of learning, or behavior, or principles of organization.

Like Step 1, this step should take place in consultation with program planners and staff--the key people you identified and contacted in Agenda A.

The extent to which you are able to sketch out and examine the rationale underlying the program will depend on your skills as a questioner. <u>This step demands that the program staff scrutinize its own thinking about the likelihood that the program it has planned will bring about its objectives.</u>

Based on your own reading and discussion about the program and the notes you took in Step 3A of Agenda A, you probably have a good idea of areas where the planners have not adequately linked the program characteristics with the intended goals. Try to focus the meeting on any "loose ends"-- planned activities that do not appear to advance the stated goals, as well as goals that are not sufficiently addressed by planned activities.

If people are likely to be defensive about the plans they have already made for a program, this may be a difficult step to complete satisfactorily. If you feel that you lack the skill to involve the staff in this sort of serious thinking, discuss the need for activities of this sort with the project director, and try to enlist her help. Perhaps she can hold a workshop, or a consultant can be brought in.

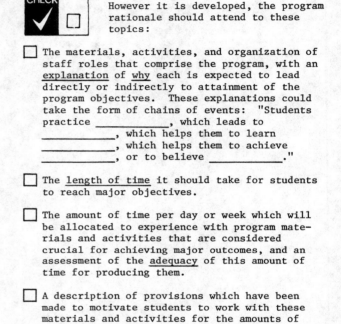 **CHECK** However it is developed, the program rationale should attend to these topics:

☐ The materials, activities, and organization of staff roles that comprise the program, with an <u>explanation</u> of <u>why</u> each is expected to lead directly or indirectly to attainment of the program objectives. These explanations could take the form of chains of events: "Students practice _____, which leads to _____, which helps them to learn _____, which helps them to achieve _____, or to believe _____."

☐ The <u>length of time</u> it should take for students to reach major objectives.

☐ The amount of time per day or week which will be allocated to experience with program materials and activities that are considered crucial for achieving major outcomes, and an assessment of the <u>adequacy</u> of this amount of time for producing them.

☐ A description of provisions which have been made to motivate students to work with these materials and activities for the amounts of time prescribed.

☐ The types of instructional <u>interactions</u> that have been planned between teachers or tutors and students to convey the important information to be learned. The description should explain why the frequency and duration of these contacts will be sufficient to produce the outcomes that are intended.

 NOTE These hard questions should be answered as specifically as possible. Few programs as initially planned attend to these critical program features in realistic enough detail.

Write the program statement

Instructions

The program statement is an in-house report, to be shared among staff members and evaluators, in which you record what you have learned about the major goals of the program as well as why and when the program as implemented is expected to achieve them. The program statement should be used as a guide for your evaluation and as a description of the program for anyone who is interested.

 How To Measure Program Implementation, Chapter 2, outlines an implementation report. The questions filling each section of the outline show the level of detail that the program statement should use to describe the program.

Try to summarize the program's major activities and materials in a table such as the following:

You might at this point also need to revise the evaluation contract you made under Agenda A. It is not unlikely that clarification of the program's components and intentions will change the staff's decision about the information they want to collect.

Table For Describing Program Implementation

Program Component:

Outcome objective addressed	Person responsible for implementation	Target group	Activity	Materials	Organization for activity (e.g., small group, individual, etc.)	Frequency/ duration	Amount of progress expected

 As the program changes and develops, you will need to periodically alter the program statement. Sometimes modifying the statement might seem an extraneous activity; but if the staff is at all interested in disseminating or enlarging the program, or announcing its benefits to the community, the program statement will serve as a constantly useful source of what to tell people.

Agenda C

Monitor Program Implementation and the Achievement of Program Objectives

Instructions

The formative evaluator serves, in a sense, as the eyes and ears of the project planners and staff--a thoughtful field agent who collects information about how the program looks at its various sites; about how students are achieving; and about how faculty, students, and parents perceive it and each other.

Agenda C encompasses the major formative function of monitoring the program's implementation, ease of installation, teacher satisfaction, and student progress. This agenda follows a fairly standard set of measurement and design procedures, although the exact nature of what you observe and communicate will, of course, vary with circumstances.

For one thing, you might be interested in monitoring implementation of the program periodically throughout, using the same instruments and procedures over and over again. In this case, times of measurement would be determined by the passage of particular time periods or by the arrival of logical milestones in the instruction--say, at the end of critical units.

On the other hand, or in addition, you could conduct more ad hoc and independent feasibility or pilot studies.* Whichever of these modes you adopt, the same principles can be used to plan data collection and construct instruments to measure implementation, attitudes, and achievement.

This agenda leads you through design and collection of formative information about the program; then Agenda D helps suggest different methods for reporting the information.

---

*If you will be able to set up a true control group, then consider using the Step-by-Step Guide for Conducting a Small Experiment, Chapter 5. That guide provides highly detailed directions for conducting a true experiment. Its relevance to your situation will be easy to judge--decide whether you can meet the five preconditions in Step 1, page 108.

Agenda C's nine steps are outlined here:

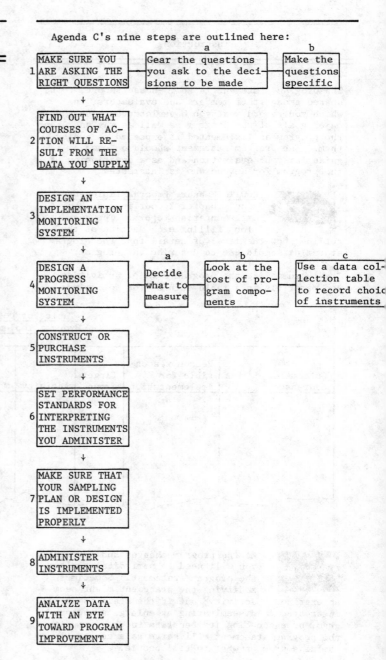

Make sure you are asking the right questions

Instructions

a. Gear the questions you ask to the decisions to be made.

Look at the agreement you have made with the program's planners. It directs you to examine different components of the program. Each monitoring activity you have agreed to engage in will need to be guided by a set of questions which reflect the decisions the program planners and staff want to make about each of these components of the program as implemented.

These questions will usually take one of three forms:

• What does Component X look like--so that it can be described?

• Does Component X look as it is supposed to-- so that it can be modified?

• Is Component X worth keeping as is?

Write down the question you want to answer about each program component you have agreed to monitor:

_____

_____

_____

The answers to questions about what the program looks like lie in measures of program implementation. How To Measure Program Implementation, Chapter 1, contains a set of questions to help you decide how much backup data you will have to collect to support your description of the program's implementation.

Answers to questions about whether a component should be changed or kept as is will lie in measures of achievement and attitudes. Specifying objectives and questions for these purposes

is discussed in How To Deal With Goals and Objectives, How To Measure Attitudes, and How To Measure Achievement.

If the issue is whether or not to keep or scrap a curriculum component, then write a question to that effect. For example, "Is the Mark-It-Up self-instructional math program worth keeping or should it be changed or discarded?"

b. Make the questions specific.

Once you have outlined important questions, your objective is to make them specific enough to suggest the measurements and comparisons to be made. Scrutinize each question, and think of how you can ask it more specifically. The question about "Mark-It-Up" might be further specified like this:

What does "worth it" mean? For the purpose of measurement, I have decided that it means:

• Students enjoy the activities

• Teachers think Mark-It-Up is beneficial

• Students pass the tests at the end of Mark-It-Up units

• Materials hold together and do not fall apart

• Instructions are clear

• Students easily learn how to use the materials

• Students make better than satisfactory progress

Check these questions with the staff to make sure that your data collection attacks their concerns as well. Refine questions accordingly.

Find out
what courses of action
will result from
the data you supply

Instructions

===

If your job is to collect information that will be
used for deciding whether to change, keep, or drop
a program component, then find out from the staff
the most likely course of action they will take if
the component proves unsatisfactory so that you
can build into the evaluation a plan to assess the
likely merits of this option as well.

 For each component you examine, have
the staff complete this statement:

"If the _____ component turns out to be
unsatisfactory, we will do _____ instead."

Whatever is entered in the second blank defines
what comparison groups should experience.

Design an implementation monitoring system

Instructions

This step has to do with finding ways to get credible information to answer the staff's questions about what the program, and its various planned or natural variations, <u>look like</u>. Your information gathering plan will have two major components:

- A set of <u>instruments</u> or other data collection methods which you have chosen to use for answering critical questions. Choice of instruments can be determined by reading <u>How To Measure Program Implementation</u>.

- A <u>sampling plan</u> or an evaluation <u>design</u> which prescribes <u>when</u> instruments will be administered, the <u>sites</u> at which this will take place, and the <u>people</u>, classes, or schools who will be the focus of this activity. <u>How To Design a Program Evaluation</u> outlines in detail six data collection plans to help you produce a credible evaluation. Pages 46 to 51 help you select an appropriate design. <u>How To Measure Program Implementation</u>, Chapter 3, describes a sampling plan for choosing sites, times to measure, and events to observe.

Summarize your plan for data collection to describe implementation and to monitor achievement, attitudes, and costs in a table like the following:

Table For Summarizing A Program Monitoring Plan

1 Instrument to be administered	2 Activity to be monitored	3 Dates of administration	4 Sites to be examined	5 Subjects of measurement

Once you have read through <u>How To Measure Program Implementation</u> or otherwise made a decision about which instruments you will use, list them--questionnaires, interviews, classroom observations, examination of program records--in Column 1 of the table. In Column 2, briefly note the name of the program implementation component--set of materials, activity, or organizational arrangement--you will examine. If accurate depiction of the component is particularly critical, then try to use more than one instrument for monitoring it.

In Column 3, list the <u>dates</u> when instruments will be administered. In Column 4, list the <u>sites</u> which you have chosen to examine. Choice of sites depends on the questions you are attempting to answer. If the program is known to vary considerably from site to site, include representatives of each version of the program in your selection. This will be particularly crucial if you are exploring the relative effects of different planned or natural variations in the program. If the program is intended to be uniform across sites, choose sites based on other criteria such as the length of time the program has been in operation at the site, the amount of experience of teachers, the characteristics of the neighborhoods involved, or the amount of funds allotted to the program. Choose as many sites as your budget will endure.

In Column 5 of the table--<u>Subjects of Measurement</u>--name the groups on whom the instruments will focus: students, teachers, parents, etc.

On a separate sheet, record the names and addresses, if necessary, of people you will need to contact in order to administer the measures. Once you have mapped out your general plan for implementation data collection, go on to pursue a similar activity regarding measurement of achievement, attitude, and costs.

If there is to be a control group, construct a data collection plan for describing what occurs to <u>it</u> while the program group is taking part in the program. If the control group is to receive <u>no</u> program, plan to verify that this is the case. If the control group is receiving a program or a component that represents an alternative the staff might adopt, then you should monitor the control group's program as carefully as that of the program group.

Instructions
---

a. Decide what to measure.

Chapter 1 of this Handbook, pages 19 to 23, offers some rules-of-thumb for deciding which measurements might be most useful to the planners and staff.

For the purpose of monitoring program achievement or the development of attitudes, try to locate already existing instruments rather than spend time constructing them from scratch. Unless your questions are so program-specific that you will not be able to find already developed measures, investigate what is available.

 The books How To Measure Achievement and How To Measure Attitudes suggest myriad sources of already existing instruments. You might use, as well, tests and questionnaires that have accompanied the program's curriculum materials.

 If you have chosen not to purchase or borrow an instrument, then How To Measure Attitudes instructs you in the design of instruments that will be useful for collecting attitude information. How To Measure Achievement contains an annotated bibliography, pages 69 to 88, which sends you to books describing methods for constructing achievement tests.

b. Look at the costs of program components if a critical factor determining the choice among program activities or indicating their relative worth is the costs they incur.

Sometimes a program component that seems to be effective might still be considered undesirable because of the large amount of money involved in purchasing or maintaining it. For formative evaluation, assess costs by keeping track of the expenses demanded for each component's continued accurate implementation over one program cycle, say, a year. Add up, therefore:

Initial cost of materials	$ _____
Cost of maintenance and repair	_____
Cost of training staff	_____
Cost of staff time spent implementing the component	_____
TOTAL	$ _____

c. Once you have chosen the instruments you will collect or design for measuring achievement, attitude, and cost outcomes of the program, note these on the same data collection table you used for summarizing your implementation data plan, Step C3.

Using the same table allows you to consolidate measures. In the interest of economy of time and money, and so that your evaluation is not intrusive on the program, try to administer only one instrument of a particular type—questionnaire, interview, achievement test, etc.—to each group of people or individual from whom you will gather data. Do not give teachers a questionnaire about program implementation and a questionnaire assessing attitudes. Pool all these questions into a single instrument.

 List in Column 1 the instruments that will be administered to monitor progress in achievement or change in attitudes. In Column 2, briefly note which activity or cognitive/affective outcome will be monitored. In Column 3, list dates when instruments will be administered. In Column 4, record the sites chosen for each data-gathering date; and in Column 5, list the people to whom instruments will be administered.

If there is a control group, list in Columns 3, 4, and 5 the dates, places, and people relevant to assessing the control group's progress.

Construct or purchase instruments

Instructions

=====

Before you begin this step, assess your resources again: Have you listed more instruments than you can realistically construct or pur-chase and administer within the time and cost confines of the evaluation? Consider the cost-cutting suggestions on page 41.

Build a schedule for obtaining instruments using this table:

Instrument Acquisition Table

1 Descrip-tion or name of instrument	2 To be con-structed or purchased (where)?	3 Person re-sponsible for purchase/con-struction	4 Date instru-ment must be received/ completed

In Column 1 of the table, name the instrument in question. In Column 2, indicate whether it is to be made in-house or purchased--and from where. Name in Column 3 the person responsible for obtaining each instrument. Column 4 shows the deadline--a date at least two weeks before its planned administration--for receipt of the com-pleted instrument. If you will have to train recorders or administrators to use the instrument, then set this date at least a month prior to its administration.

Set performance standards for interpreting the instruments you administer

---

Instructions

Before administering any measure to collect formative information, talk with the staff and <u>decide how results will be interpreted</u>. When information you collect is reported to the staff, it will need to be interpreted and acted upon. For this reason, some preset notion of <u>good performance</u> will need to be established.

Ask the staff to refer to their answers to questions you asked about good and poor performance during Agenda B, page 50. Then ask these questions regarding <u>program implementation</u>:

☐ How much deviation from the established plan are you willing to tolerate?

☐ Which components of the program do you insist be implemented exactly as planned? Which will you allow to vary fairly freely?

Ask these questions about <u>achievement and attitudes</u>:

☐ How much of a difference between the program and control groups will you want to see before declaring the program successful?

☐ What sorts of norm scores will indicate to you successful performance?

☐ What scores on the instruments to be administered will indicate to you satisfactory, middling, or unsatisfactory performance? Answering this will be particularly useful. After dividing the potential score range from each instrument into appropriate categories-- high, average, and poor; or mastery and non- mastery--determine the <u>percent of students</u> (or other cases) whose scores (or mean scores) should fall into the highest category and the largest tolerable percentage who can score low. Decisions to revise will be based on how closely actual achievement matches these standards.

<u>How To Measure Achievement</u>, pages 142 and 143, describes in greater detail the use of such standards for inter- preting test data. In addition, Chapter 6 discusses the types of scores your instruments might produce, with suggestions for presenting them to audiences for formative eval- uation.

If you have not planned to use a control group, reconsider now. Con- sult Chapter 1 of <u>How To Design a Program Evaluation</u> for ideas about using control group and time series designs for formative evaluation. Chapter 1 describes some evaluation designs, some of them fairly unorthodox, which might be useful for formative evaluation.

<u>Using a control group increases the interpreta- bility of formative information by providing a basis of comparison from which to judge the results that you obtain</u>. Having a preset basis from which to judge results will make it easy for the staff to decide what to do about the informa- tion you report.

Make sure that your sampling plan or design is implemented properly

---

Instructions

CHECK ✓ ☐   If you are working with a <u>control group</u> design, look at the table below and complete the checklist to make sure you have properly implemented the design.

<u>Checklist for a Control Group Design</u>
<u>With Pretest</u>

1. Name the person responsible for setting up the design_____

<u>If the design uses a true control group:</u>

2. Will there be blocking? ☐ yes ☐ no

   (See <u>How To Design a Program Evaluation</u>, page 149.)

3. If yes, based upon what?
   ☐ ability   ☐ sex
   ☐ achievement   ☐ other_____

4. Has randomization been completed?
   ☐ yes ☐ no   Date_____

<u>If the design uses a non-equivalent control group:</u>

5. Name this group_____

6. List the major differences between the program and comparison groups (e.g., sex, SES, ability, time of day of class, geographical location, age):

   _____
   _____
   _____

7. Contact made to secure cooperation of comparison group? ☐

   Date_____

8. Agreement received from (Ms./Mr.)_____

9. Agreement was in the form of (letter/memo/ personal conversation/etc.)_____

---

10. Confirmatory letter or memo sent? ☐
    Date_____

11. List of students assigned to program is on file (where?)_____

<u>In either event:</u>

12. Name of pretest_____

13. Pretest completed? ☐   Date_____

14. Teachers (or other program implementors) warned:
    ☐ To avoid confounds? Memo sent or meeting held (date)_____
    ☐ To avoid contamination? Memo sent or meeting held (date)_____

    (See <u>How To Design a Program Evaluation</u>, page 60.)

15. Check made that both programs will span the same time period? ☐   Date_____

16. Posttest given? ☐   Date_____

17. List of possible confounds and contaminations
    _____
    _____
    _____

 CHECK ✓ ☐   If you are using a <u>time series design</u>, use this table to make sure you have attended to everything.

<u>Time Series Design</u>
<u>(With Optional Non-Equivalent Control)</u>
<u>Group Checklist</u>

1. Name of person responsible for setting up and maintaining design_____

2. Name of instruments to be administered and readministered_____

   _____

3. Equivalent form of instruments to be:
   ☐ Made in house   ☐ Purchased

4. Number of repeated measurements to be made per instrument_____

5. Dates of planned measurements:

    ☐ 1st_____   ☐ 5th_____

    ☐ 2nd_____   ☐ 6th_____

    ☐ 3rd_____   additional:

    ☐ 4th_____   ☐ _____

If the design uses a control group:

6. Name of control group_____

7. List of major differences between the program group and the control group (e.g., sex, SES, ability, geographical location, age):

    _____

    _____

8. Contact made to secure cooperation of comparison group? ☐   Date_____

9. Agreement received from (Ms./Mr.)_____

10. Confirmatory letter or memo sent? ☐

    Date_____

11. List of possible contaminations and confounds

    _____

    _____

    _____

3. How many cases will be sampled from each cell?_____ (see How To Design a Program Evaluation, pages 157-161, for suggestions about selecting random samples)

4. Cases selected? ☐

5. For each time selected:

    Have instruments been administered? ☐

    Comments_____

    What deviations from the sampling plan have occurred?_____

    _____

CHECK ✓ ☐   The following table includes a checklist for implementing a sampling plan for collecting implementation and progress data from a representative sample of sites, times, and people. Use this checklist to guide your implementation of the sampling plan.

Sampling Plan Checklist

1. The sample will ensure adequate representation to different types of:

    ☐ Sites (what kinds?)_____

    ☐ Time periods (which ones?)_____

    ☐ Program units (which ones?)_____

    ☐ Program roles (which ones?)_____

    ☐ Student or staff characteristics (name them)_____

    ☐ Other_____

2. The sampling plan comprises a matrix cube with _____ cells (see How To Measure Program Implementation, pages 60 to 65)

Administer instruments

Instructions

A table like the following should
help you keep track of instrument
development, administration,
scoring, and data recording.

Instrument	Completion/ Receipt Deadline	Administration Deadlines				Scoring Deadline	√?	Recording Deadline	√?
		pre	√?	post	√?				

Each of the How To Measure books in
the <u>Program Evaluation Kit</u> contains
suggestions for administering the
instruments you are using as well as
detailed directions for recording, scoring, and
summarizing their results:

• In <u>How To Measure Achievement</u>, see pages 117-145.

• In <u>How To Measure Attitudes</u>, see pages 159-177.

• In <u>How To Measure Program Implementation</u>, see
  pages 60-77.

Instructions

If you are periodically monitoring the program--
and particularly if there is a control group--then
you have collected a battery of
general measures that can be analyzed using fairly standard statistical methods. Consider whether
you will:

☐ Graph results from the various instruments

☐ Perform tests of the statistical significance
of differences in performance among groups or
from a single group's pretest and posttest

☐ Calculate correlations to look for relationships

☐ Compute indices of inter-rater reliability

How To Measure Achievement discusses
using test results for statistical
analysis on pages 125 to 145. How
To Measure Attitudes describes
attitude test scores used for calculating statistics on pages 170 to 177. See, as well, How To
Measure Program Implementation, pages 67 to 77.
Problems of calculating inter-rater reliability
are discussed in all three books. Specific
statistical analyses are discussed in How To
Calculate Statistics.

All of the Kit's How To books contain suggestions
for building graphs and tables to summarize
results. For each instrument you use, see the
relevant How To book. Consult, as well, Chapter 4
of How To Present an Evaluation Report.

Remember that in addition to describing program implementation and
the progress in development of
skills and attitudes of various
participants, you may also need to note whether
the program is keeping pace with the time schedule
that has been mapped out.

If you have focused data collection on specific
program units, or if you are conducting pilot
tests, then in addition to performing statistical
analyses, consider whether the program has
achieved each of the objectives in question.
In particular, examine these things:

- Student achievement
- Participants' attitudes about the program com-
  ponent in question
- The component's implementation

Below you will find four cases describing results
you might obtain, with suggestions about what to
do about each. Determinations of good, poor, and
adequate performance should be based on the performance standards set in Step 6.

Case 1

- Achievement test results: good
- Program implementation: adequate
- Attitude results: poor

What to do? Check the technical quality of the
instrument (see How To Measure Attitudes,
pages 131 to 151). Find out what is causing bad
morale:

☐ Is the program too easy? Pretest students for
upcoming program units to see if they have
already mastered some of the objectives.

☐ Is the program too difficult? If this complaint is widespread, try to alleviate the
pressure of the work.

☐ Is this part of the program dull? The response
to this depends on the students and subject
matter. Try to find motivators for the students, or help teachers to invent ways to make
instruction more appealing and relevant. If
minor changes offer no promise, the staff is
convinced of the importance of program objectives, and the rest of the program seems more
interesting, then don't revise.

Case 2

- Achievement test results: good
- Program implementation: poor
- Attitude results: good

What to do? First ask:

☐ Did the achievement test and the program component address the same objectives? <u>If not</u>, there's your answer! <u>If so</u>, check the technical quality of the implementation measure. See <u>How To Measure Program Implementation</u>, pages 129 to 138.

Then ask:

☐ What happened in the program instead of what was planned? Make sure that students did not learn from the mistakes they made while struggling through poor instruction. If possible, suggest that the instruction that <u>did</u> occur become officially part of the program.

<u>Case 3</u>

• Achievement test results: poor
• Program implementation: good
• Attitude results: good

What to do? First ask:

☐ Did students misinterpret test items in some way, and if so, how?

Then assure yourself that the objective underlying the test matches the objective underlying the instruction. If so, examine the technical quality of the achievement test. See <u>How To Measure Achievement</u>, pages 89 to 115.

Then ask:

☐ Was student performance during program implementation good? If so, check whether the <u>amount of practice</u> given to students was sufficient to allow them to master the objective.

☐ Was student performance on program tasks poor? If so, explore whether sufficient time was given for practice <u>and</u> whether students lacked <u>prerequisite</u> skills necessary to learn the material. You may need to give diagnostic tests to locate students' skill deficiencies. Check to see whether the instruction itself was difficult or confusing. Did students understand what was expected of them?

<u>Case 4</u>

More than two of the indicators show unsatisfactory results. In any of these cases, you should investigate the cause of the problem and revise as necessary.

Instructions

The key to an effective formative evaluation is good communication. Information about where the program is or is not working needs to be timely and clearly presented.

Agenda D has three steps:

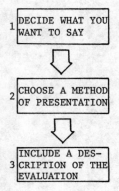

1 | DECIDE WHAT YOU WANT TO SAY

2 | CHOOSE A METHOD OF PRESENTATION

3 | INCLUDE A DESCRIPTION OF THE EVALUATION

Decide what you want to say

Instructions

You want to get the information across quickly and succinctly. Therefore think about each instrument you have administered and:

☐ Make a graph or table summarizing the major quantitative findings you want to report. How To Calculate Statistics, pages 18 to 25, describes how to graph test scores.

☐ Check How To Present an Evaluation Report, Chapters 1 and 2, for suggestions about organizing your message and an outline of an evaluation report. Look over the outline and decide which of the topics apply to your report. If you will need to describe program implementation, look at the report outline in Chapter 2 of How To Measure Program Implementation.

☐ Write a quick general outline of what you plan to discuss.

If you are submitting an interim report for a program that is being assembled from scratch, you should include in Section II of the report a few paragraphs dealing with progress in program design. They might be entitled, for instance, Materials Production or Staff Development. The paragraphs should address these questions:

☐ Has research been conducted to determine the sort of curriculum that is appropriate to the program? Who conducted this research? How useful has it been?

☐ What materials development has been promised for the program? For which objectives? For which sites? What student materials? Any teacher manuals? Any teacher training materials? Any audiovisuals? Has the staff promised to expand or revise something previously existing? Did they submit in the proposal an outline, plan, or prototype of the promised materials? Are the materials being produced in accordance with this? Have there been changes? Has the staff decided to

not develop something they promised? Why? How is development of these particular materials progressing? Is it on schedule? Behind? Why? Does the staff plan to catch up by year's end, or is this unnecessary because they are well ahead of student progress? How much of the intended materials development will be completed by the end of the evaluation?

☐ What staff development and training have been provided to ensure that planners, teachers, etc., are equal to the tasks of both designing and implementing a new program?

☐ What plans for staff member participation in materials development are contained in the proposal? Is this an accurate description of what has occurred so far?

☐ What staff-community interchanges to gather help with planning were mentioned in the proposal? What staff meetings—within the project or with staff members outside it—were planned? Did these occur? What were their purposes and outcomes?

Step 2

Choose a method of presentation

If the manner of reporting was not negotiated during Agenda A, decide whether your report to each audience will be oral or written, formal or informal.

 Chapter 3 of How To Present an Evaluation Report lists a set of pointers to help you organize what you intend to say and decide how to say it.

Step 3

Include a description of the evaluation

 Follow the outline described in Chapter 2 of How To Present an Evaluation Report, Section III. The report should include:

• A description of why you undertook the evaluation

• Who the decision-makers were

• The kinds of formative questions you intended to ask, the evaluation designs you used, if any, and the instruments you used to measure implementation, achievement, and attitudes

• Less formal data collection methods which you used

If you have found instruments which were particularly useful, or sensitive to detecting the implementation or effects of the particular program, put them in an appendix.

Your report should conclude, importantly, with suggestions to the summative evaluator, if indeed a summative evaluation of this particular program will be conducted.

This is the end of the Step-by-Step Guides for Conducting a Formative Evaluation. By now evaluation is a familiar topic to you and, hopefully, a growing interest. These guides are designed to be used again and again. Perhaps you will want to use them in the future, each time trying a more elaborate design and more sophisticated measures. Evaluation is a new field. Be assured that people evaluating programs--yourself included--are breaking new ground.

Chapter 4

Step-by-Step Guide For Conducting a Summative Evaluation

The summative evaluator of an educational program has responsibility for producing an accurate description of the program—complete with measures of its effects—that summarizes what has transpired during a particular time period. Results from a summative evaluation, usually compiled into a written report, can be used for several purposes:

- To document for the funding agency that services promised by the program's planners have indeed been delivered
- To assure that a lasting record of the program remains on file
- To serve as a planning document for people who want to duplicate the program or adapt it to another setting

The step-by-step guide in this chapter presents the steps to be taken in conducting the summative evaluation of an educational program. While the exact procedures to be followed when accomplishing such an evaluation will vary with the setting, summative evaluation in general includes the tasks and follows the sequence described here. The novice to evaluation, for whom this guide is primarily intended, will therefore do well to follow the guide.

This step-by-step guide divides summative evaluation into five *phases*, each corresponding to a major task to be accomplished:

Phase A   Focus the Evaluation—that is, decide what needs to be known, and by whom
Phase B   Select Appropriate Measures
Phase C   Collect Data
Phase D   Analyze Data
Phase E   Prepare an Evaluation Report

These five phases will occur in a fixed order, regardless of the content of the evaluation, although what you do during the early phases will often be determined by your plans about how to conduct later ones. Which tests and measures you select during Phase B, for example, will depend on the resources available for data analysis and the information you intend to report later on. This means that many of the decisions guiding the evaluation will need to be made early.

Whenever possible, the step-by-step guide uses checklists and worksheets to help you keep track of what you have decided and found out. Actually, the worksheets might be better called "guidesheets," since you will have to copy many of them onto your own paper rather than use the one in the book. Space simply does not permit the book to provide places to list large quantities of data.

As you use the guide, you will come upon references marked by the symbol ✏. These direct you to read sections of various *How To* books contained in the *Program Evaluation Kit*. At these junctures in the evaluation, it will be necessary for you to review a concept or follow a procedure outlined in one of these seven resource books.

- *How To Deal With Goals and Objectives*
- *How To Design a Program Evaluation*
- *How To Measure Program Implementation*
- *How To Measure Attitudes*
- *How To Measure Achievement*
- *How To Calculate Statistics*
- *How To Present an Evaluation Report*

To give you an overview of the summative evaluation tasks included in the guide, flow charts showing the steps required to complete each phase appear in the introduction to each.

The focusing or general planning phase of a summative evaluation is crucial and often difficult.
It is a time when you read important documents,
talk to people, and think through the whole evaluation. You decide what you <u>do</u> and <u>don't</u> need to
know, so that the evaluation you finally carry out
is useful to your audiences, accurate in its description of the program, and efficiently carried
out. In summative evaluation, once you have completed this focusing, or conceptualizing, the rest
should be straight-sailing.

The three steps and six substeps in Phase A can
be summarized by this flowchart:

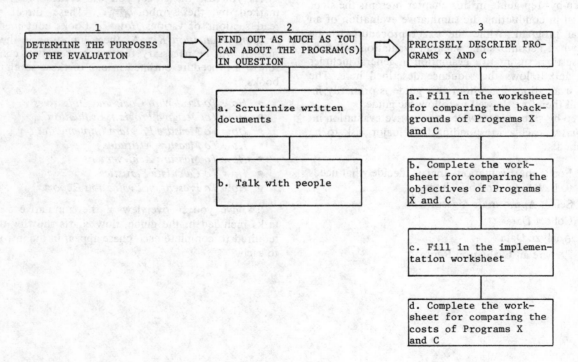

1
DETERMINE THE PURPOSES OF THE EVALUATION

2
FIND OUT AS MUCH AS YOU CAN ABOUT THE PROGRAM(S) IN QUESTION

a. Scrutinize written documents

b. Talk with people

3
PRECISELY DESCRIBE PROGRAMS X AND C

a. Fill in the worksheet for comparing the backgrounds of Programs X and C

b. Complete the worksheet for comparing the objectives of Programs X and C

c. Fill in the implementation worksheet

d. Complete the worksheet for comparing the costs of Programs X and C

Determine the purposes of the evaluation

Instructions

The job of the summative evaluator is to collect, digest, and report information about a program to satisfy the needs of one or more audiences. The audiences in turn might use the information for either of three purposes:

- To learn about the program

- To satisfy themselves that the program they were promised did indeed occur and if not, what happened instead

- To make decisions about continuing or discontinuing, expanding or limiting the program, generally through giving or withholding funds

If a <u>decision</u> hinges on your findings, your first job is to find out what the decision is. Then you will have to ensure that you collect the appropriate information and report it to the correct audiences.

 Begin your descriptions of the decisions to be made and your audience(s) by answering the following questions:

☐ What is the title of the program to be evaluated?_____

_____

<u>Throughout this chapter, this program will be referred to as Program X.</u>

☐ What decisions will be based on the evaluation? _____
_____

☐ Who wants to know about the program? That is, who is the evaluation's audience?

- Teachers_____

  Report due_____

- Administrators_____

  Report due_____

- Counselors or department heads_____

  Report due_____

- District Personnel_____

  Report due_____

- School Board_____

  Report due_____

- Superintendent_____

  Report due_____

- State Department of Education_____

  Report due_____

- Federal Personnel_____

  Report due_____

- Parents_____

  Report due_____

- Community in general_____

  Report due_____

- Other--special interest groups, for instance

  _____

  Report due_____

 Try not to serve too many audiences at once. To produce a credible summative evaluation, your position must allow you to be objective. See pages 15 and 16 of this <u>Handbook</u> for elaboration of this critical admonition.

Ask the people who constitute your primary audience this question:

☐ What would be done if Program X were to be found inadequate?

_____

_____

_____

Here name <u>another program</u> or the <u>old program</u>, or indicate that they would have <u>no program at all</u>. What you enter in this blank is the alternative with which Program X should be compared. There could be many alternatives or competitors; but select the <u>most likely</u> alternative.

<u>This most-likely-alternative-to-Program-X, its</u>
<u>closest competitor, is referred to throughout</u>
<u>this guide as Program C.</u> Write it after the
word "or" in the next sentence:

A choice must be made between continuing Program X <u>or</u> . . .

_____

_____

This is Program C.

<u>If at all possible, set up or locate a control or</u>
<u>comparison group which receives Program C.</u>

 Consult Chapter 1 of <u>How To Design a</u>
<u>Program Evaluation</u> for ideas about
using control group designs. Chapter 1 describes evaluation designs,
some of them fairly unorthodox, which might be
useful for situations where control groups are
difficult to set up. Using a control group
greatly increases the interpretability of your
information by providing a basis of comparison
from which to judge the results that you obtain.
Pages 24 to 32 of the same book describe different
sets of control groups and the programs they
might receive.

☐ Has one of the evaluation's audiences, such as
  a Federal or State funding agency, stated
  specific requirements for this evaluation? Are
  you required, for instance, to use particular
  tests, to measure attainment of particular outcomes, or to report on special forms? If so,
  summarize these evaluation requirements by
  quoting or referencing the documents that
  stipulate them.

_____

_____

_____

_____

_____

 What is the absolute deadline for
the earliest evaluation report?
Record the <u>earliest</u> of the dates you
listed when describing audiences.

The Evaluation Report must be ready by_____.

Find out as much as you can about the program(s) in question

Instructions

a. <u>Scrutinize written documents</u> that describe Program X, Program C, or both:

CHECK ✓ ☐

☐ A program <u>proposal</u> written for the funding agency

☐ The request for proposals (RFP) written by the sponsor or funding agency to which this program's proposal was a response

☐ Results of a needs assessment* whose findings the program is intended to address

☐ Written state or district guidelines about program processes and goals to which this program must conform

☐ The program's <u>budget</u>, particularly the part that mentions the evaluation

☐ A description of, or an organizational chart depicting, the administrative and staff roles played by various people in the program

☐ Curriculum guides for the materials which have been purchased for the program

☐ Past evaluations of this or similar programs

☐ Lists of goals and objectives which the staff or planners feel describe the program's aims

☐ Tests or surveys which the program planners feel could be used to measure the effects of the program, such as a district-wide year end assessment instrument

☐ Tests or surveys that were used by the program's formative evaluator, if there was one

☐ Memos, meeting minutes, newspaper articles-- descriptions made by the staff or the planners of the program

☐ Descriptions of the program's history, or of the social context into which it has been designed to fit

*A needs assessment is an announcement of educational needs, expressed in terms of the school curriculum and policies, by representatives of the school or district constituency.

☐ Articles in the education and evaluation literature that describe the effects of programs such as the one in question, its curricular materials, or its various subcomponents

☐ Other_____

Once you have discovered which materials are available, seek them out and copy them if possible.

Take notes in the margins. Write down, or dictate onto tape, comments about your general impression of the program, its context, and staff. This will get you started on writing your own description of the program. You may want to complete Step 3 concurrently with this general overview. Be alert, in particular, for the following details:

☐ The program's major general goals. List separately those that seem to be of highest priority to planners, the community, or the program's sponsors. Note where these priorities differ across audiences, since your report to each should reflect the priorities of each.

☐ Specifically stated objectives

☐ The philosophy or point of view of the program planners and sponsors, if these differ

☐ Examples of similar programs that planners intend to emulate

☐ Writers in the field of education whose point of view the program is intended to mirror

☐ The <u>needs</u> of the community or constituency which the program is intended to meet—whether these have been explictly stated or seem to implicitly underly the program

_____

_____

☐ Program implementation directives and requirements, described in the proposal, required by the sponsor, or both

_____

_____

☐ The amount of variation tolerated by the program from site to site, or even student to student

_____

_____

☐ The number and distribution of sites involved

_____

_____

☐ Canned or prepublished curricula to be used for the program

_____

_____

☐ Curriculum materials to be constructed in-house

_____

_____

☐ Plans which have been developed describing how the program looks in operation—times of day, scripts for lessons, etc.

_____

_____

☐ Administrative, decision-making, and teaching <u>roles</u> played by various people

_____

_____

☐ Staff responsibilities

_____

_____

☐ Descriptions of extra-instructional requirements placed on the program, such as the need to obtain parental permissions or to include teacher training or community outreach activities

_____

_____

☐ Student evaluation plans

_____

_____

☐ Teacher evaluation plans

_____

_____

☐ Program evaluation plans

_____

_____

☐ Descriptions of program aspirations that have been stated as percents of students achieving certain objectives and/or deadlines by which particular objectives should be reached

_____

_____

b. Check with people

Check your description of the program against the impressions and aspirations of your audiences and the program's planners and staff. By all means, contact the people who will be in the best position to <u>use</u> the information you collect, your primary audience.

Try to think at this time of <u>other</u> people whose actions, opinions, and decisions will influence the success of the evaluation and the extent to which the information you collect will be useful and used. Make sure that you talk with each of these people, either at a group meeting or individually. Seek out in particular:

☐ Evaluators who have worked with this particular program or programs like it. They will have valuable advice to give about what information to collect, how, and from whom.

☐ School or district personnel not directly connected with the project, but whose cooperation will help you carry out the evaluation more efficiently or quickly. <u>Negotiate access to the programs</u>!

☐ Influential parents or community members whose support will help the evaluation go more smoothly

If key people are too busy to talk, send them memos. Describe the evaluation, what you would like them to do for you, and when.

NOTE If possible, observe the program in operation or programs like it. Take a field trip in the company of program planners and staff. Have them point out the program's key components and major variations.

Take careful notes of everything you see and hear. Later you may find some of these valuable.

Precisely describe Programs X and C

Instructions

In this step, outline the distinctive features of Program X and that received by the competitor or control group you have chosen to use, Program C. Of course, if there will be <u>no</u> competitor, you will not have to fill in the boxes that refer to it.

Writing this section will also help you rough out the introductory sections of the eventual evaluation report.

<u>How To Present an Evaluation Report</u>, Chapter 2, contains an outline of what you should include in your description of the goals and primary characteristics of the program. <u>How To Measure Program Implementation</u>, Chapter 2, lists in detail questions to answer in your description of how the program looks.

If both Program X and Program C are likely contenders for adoption, then <u>both</u> are the foci of the evaluation. Both should be described in the greatest detail possible. If Program C is <u>no</u> program or one that is not an alternative to X, then describe what happens to the control group generally, with a focus on chances its members might have to pick up what Program X teaches.

Worksheets like the following will help you organize your description of the program.

a. <u>Fill in the worksheet for comparing the backgrounds of Programs X and C</u>

CHECK ☑ ☐   BACKGROUNDS WORKSHEET

☐ Program C will be the closest competitor of Program X

☐ Program C will be a control group receiving either no program or one that is not a contender

---

☐ There will be <u>no</u> competitor or control group

- Title of Program X _____
  Title of Program C _____
- Sites of Program X _____
  Sites of Program C _____

People Affected by Programs X and C

<u>Parents</u>

- Is parent permission needed for son or daughter to participate in Program X? _____
  In Program C? _____

- Were parents to be actively involved in the program activities in X? ☐   C? ☐
  Were they to have an advisory role in X? ☐
  C? ☐

<u>Staff</u>

- Who are the teachers for Program X?
  _____
  _____

  Who are the teachers for Program C?
  _____
  _____

- What characteristics are required of teachers employed in Program X, e.g., language abilities, subject area skills, teaching experience, in-service training?
  _____
  _____

  In Program C?
  _____
  _____

• Administrators involved in Program X?

_____

_____

In Program C?

_____

_____

• Other staff?

Aides in Program X?_____

Aides in Program C?_____

Secretaries in Program X?_____

Secretaries in Program C?_____

Others in Program X?_____

Others in Program C?_____

• Consultants or other specialists for Program X?

_____

_____

For Program C?

_____

_____

Program Origins

• How did Program X get started?

_____

_____

Was there a needs assessment?_____

How did Program C get started?

_____

_____

Was there a needs assessment?_____

• Official demands on the programs

What legal or funding demands or restrictions have been place on Program X?

_____

_____

On Program C?

_____

_____

Note where background characteristics of the programs--for instance, relative experience of teachers-- might reduce the comparability of Programs X and C.

_____

_____

_____

 Complete the worksheet for comparing the objectives of Programs X and C to help you clarify what you expect to be the results or outcomes of the two programs.

 Details of method and purpose regarding this step are discussed at length in How To Deal With Goals and Objectives. That book suggests alternative ways to state objectives suitable as bases for an evaluation. These directions, and the list in Chapter 2 of available objectives collections, should be useful if you find that the program's objectives are too vague to suggest what to measure.

 List the desired outcomes of Program X on the worksheet below. Try to make at least one entry in each blank; this will help you think of outcomes that you might not have otherwise considered. Leave blanks empty only where you think listing outcomes would be totally irrelevant.

NOTE Keep careful track of how closely the competitor or control group's desired outcomes correspond with those of Program X. If Program C is a competitor to Program X rather than a control group, then the two programs probably strive for quite a few of the same outcomes. If Program C is a no-program control group, then possibly none of its desired outcomes coincide with Program X. This is OK for now. It should be taken into account, however, when you interpret your results.

OBJECTIVES WORKSHEET

Desired Outcomes of Program X: Cognitive and Psychomotor

• At the end of Program X, the students will have learned_____

_____

• At the end of Program X, the teachers will have learned_____

_____

• At the end of Program X, the parents will have learned_____

_____

• At the end of Program X, community members will have learned_____

_____

• At the end of Program X, others will have learned_____

_____

Desired Outcomes of Program C: Cognitive and Psychomotor

- At the end of Program C, the <u>students</u> will have learned_____

_____

- At the end of Program C, the <u>teachers</u> will have learned_____

_____

- At the end of Program C, the <u>parents</u> will have learned_____

_____

- At the end of Program C, <u>community members</u> will have learned_____

_____

- At the end of Program C, <u>others</u> will have learned_____

_____

Desired Outcomes of Program X: Affective/Attitudinal

- At the end of Program X, the <u>students</u> will have the following attitude(s)_____

_____

- At the end of Program X, the <u>teachers</u> will have the following attitude(s)_____

_____

- At the end of Program X, the <u>parents</u> will have the following attitude(s)_____

_____

- At the end of Program X, <u>community members</u> will have the following attitude(s)_____

_____

- At the end of Program X, <u>others</u> will have the following attitude(s)_____

_____

Desired Outcomes of Program C: Affective/Attitudinal

- At the end of Program C, the <u>students</u> will have the following attitude(s)_____

_____

- At the end of Program C, the <u>teachers</u> will have the following attitude(s)_____

_____

- At the end of Program C, the <u>parents</u> will have the following attitude(s)_____

_____

- At the end of Program C, <u>community members</u> will have the following attitude(s)_____

_____

- At the end of Program C, <u>others</u> will have the following attitude(s)_____

_____

Other Desired Outcomes of Program X: political, organizational, social, etc.

_____

_____

_____

Other Desired Outcomes of Program C: political, organizational, social, etc.

_____

_____

_____

Now, go back and <u>make sure</u> that outcomes desired by your audiences --particularly the funding agency-- appear on the lists of outcomes you just completed.

Do you need to meet with or poll your audiences to find out more exactly what they want to know, what they already know, and what <u>their</u> goals are for the program? If so, now is the time to do so. Use the <u>outcomes</u> listed in the step to structure your meeting. Amend it according to the decisions made there. Add and subtract outcomes if necessary.

Once you are sure that all the desired outcomes are listed on the outcomes chart, go back over it and <u>rank the outcomes you have listed</u> in order of importance--#1 will be <u>the most crucial outcome that the programs are supposed to achieve</u>, #2 the next most important, and so forth. This ranking will serve as a guide to planning what to measure in Phase B.

If you need help with ranking outcomes, consult <u>How To Deal With Goals and Objectives</u>, Chapter 4.

C. <u>Fill in the implementation worksheet</u>. It describes the materials, resources, and activities that comprise Programs X and C.

The purpose of this worksheet is to help you define the materials, activities, and organizational arrangements that are crucial to the implementation of the programs you are comparing.

Once these activities are defined, you can give some thought to how you will measure their accurate execution. Although different programs place various amounts of emphasis on exact execution of particular activities, virtually all of them specify <u>some</u> activities that are to take place. In fact, some--such as open classrooms-- might focus more closely on appropriate installation of materials and activities than upon immediate achievement of outcomes.

In any case, list those materials and activities that you or the program planners feel are most crucial to proper carrying out of Programs X and C.

List the most crucial materials and activities of Programs X and C in the table below. Of course, if there will be no competitor or control group, then write <u>no program</u> over the Program C questions.

IMPLEMENTATION WORKSHEET

<u>Resources</u>

• New instructional materials introduced for Program X_____

_____

_____

For Program C_____

_____

_____

• Old instructional materials retained for Program X_____

_____

For Program C_____

_____

• Equipment--projectors, lab sinks, etc.--purchased for Program X_____

_____

For Program C_____

_____

• Facilities--number of classrooms, etc.--allotted for Program X_____

_____

For Program C_____

_____

• Time allotted to Program X per day

_____

Time allotted to Program C per day

_____

• Other--Program X_____

Other--Program C_____

_____

<u>Activities</u>

Crucial activities and materials in Program X	A stranger who came upon the activity in operation or the materials in use would see...		
	Students doing this:	Teachers doing this:	Others doing this:
1.			
2.			
3.			
etc.			

Crucial activities and materials in Program C	A stranger who came upon the activity in operation or the materials in use would see...		
	Students doing this:	Teachers doing this:	Others doing this:
1.			
2.			
3.			
etc.			

Consult, as well, Chapter 2 of <u>How To Measure Program Implementation</u>. It lists questions to ask the staff and planners of both programs to help them describe implementation in detail.

If it falls within your job role to <u>critique</u> the programs as well as describe them and their relative effectiveness, then at this point make a judgment about the clarity and coherence of each program's <u>goals</u> and <u>rationale</u>. Ask yourself:

• Are the goals and objectives stated precisely enough to be understood by the program's staff and constituency?

- Or are they so unclear that they detract from the program's sense of common purpose?

- Is the <u>rationale</u> underpinning either program logical or well-thought-out?

- Or is there confusion or misunderstanding about <u>why</u> the program's activities should lead to its intended outcomes?

 d. <u>Complete the worksheet for comparing the costs of Programs X and C</u>

The purpose of this worksheet is to help you clarify informally the <u>costs</u> you want to check in order to evaluate Programs X and C. These costs could be <u>qualitative</u>, such as drains on the teachers' energy, and <u>dollar</u> costs such as the cost of materials. <u>Both</u> Program X and Program C will have associated costs.

List below three or four possible major costs brought about by each program.

 Be careful when delineating costs to differentiate <u>start-up</u> costs from <u>continuation</u> costs. Start-up costs occur at the beginning of the program. Some quantitative start-up costs might result from purchasing materials, training, etc. A qualitative start-up cost might be poor morale due to initial disorganization. Start-up costs, unless they are massive and unlikely to diminish the next time the program occurs, will likely be of less interest in summative evaluation than continuation costs. These latter are incurred by day-to-day program operation--for instance, salaries, chronic materials replacement, or poor attitudes.

 Look over the costs and benefits worksheet, and check those costs which will be one-time-only.

 <u>How To Present an Evaluation Report</u>, pages 24 and 25, lists some additional questions to consider when preparing to measure costs.

COSTS WORKSHEET	
Expected Costs-- <u>Qualitative</u> List here qualitative non-money costs that might occur such as extra fatigue. Do not forget <u>opportunity costs</u> of each program--that is, good things foregone in order to implement the program. Be careful to also list possible negative effects of each program on <u>those not in the program</u>, such as resentment, increased class size, etc.	Expected Costs-- <u>Dollars</u> List here those facets of each program that will require spending <u>extra</u> dollars--dollars that might have been spent as a matter of course if the program were not implemented. <u>Estimate</u> these costs when costs can be more exactly determined.
The following negative consequences might occur as a result of Program X _____ _____ _____	The following amount of money will be spent over and above what is usually spent as a result of Program X _____ _____ _____
The following negative consequences might occur as a result of Program C _____ _____ _____	The following amount of money will be spent over and above what is usually spent as a result of Program C _____ _____ _____

Phase B
Select Appropriate Measurements and Evaluation Designs

Instructions

In Phase A, Focus the Evaluation, you made three decisions determining the form of the evaluation you are conducting:

- You acquainted yourself with the uses to which the information you collect will be put.

- You decided whether the evaluation will involve a competitor or a control group.

- You made tentative lists of outcomes, activities, and costs that you might measure to gauge the success of the program of interest relative to the control program, if any.

In Phase B, you narrow down the list of outcomes, costs, and activities to the ones that are most crucial and easily measured within your time and money constraints. Then you:

- Select instruments to measure them.

- Choose an evaluation design, based partly on your access to control groups, for each measure you will administer. Probably just one or two designs will underlie the whole evaluation.

- Rough out a ballpark estimate of how much your evaluation will cost--and trim accordingly.

Phase B's eight steps and seven substeps can occur simultaneously. Their most usual sequence, however, is described in this flowchart:

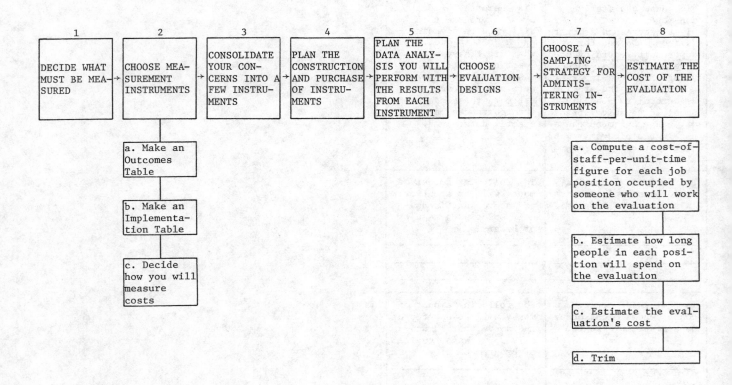

Decide what must be measured

Instructions

In Phase A you described three sets of features of both Program X and its competitor Program C:

- The planned outcomes common to both--Step 3b

- The activities crucial to the implementation of each--Step 3c

- The costs of each--Step 3d

These three lists offer a wealth of measurement possibilities. The purpose of this step is to help you decide which outcomes, implementation aspects, and costs will be most useful for you to measure. Of course, it would be nice if you could measure whether all the activities have been implemented as planned, and what the actual costs of the program were. But there is probably not sufficient time and money to allow this.

Instead, you will have to shorten the list.

Which outcomes? Look at the Objectives Worksheet in Step 3b, beginning on page 76. It lists the desired outcomes of Programs X and C in order of priority. For now, simply circle the most important ones that are common to both programs--the ones you know you will need to discuss plus others that might interest you for other reasons.

Which activities? While it is important to make sure that the programs looked as they were planned to look, what you describe about each program --as well as which aspects of your description you decide to support with backup data --will vary according to your role and the situation.

Chapter 1 of How To Measure Program Implementation asks questions to help you decide which of the features listed in the Implementation Worksheet, page 78, you should document.

Which costs? Dollar costs listed on the Costs Worksheet, page 79, will not be hard to measure; you can consult your records for this. Plan to measure all the dollar costs of Programs X and C, if it is a competitor. Qualitative costs will be more difficult both to define and to measure but circle two that you plan to measure per program. Number them 1 and 2 in order of priority.

Consult Chapter 1 of this Handbook, pages 19 to 23, for additional discussion on the topic of what to measure.

If at all possible, meet with members of your audiences and ask them to help you complete this step and the following one.

It is critical that you devote your resources to finding out what the audience most wants to know.

Choose measurement instruments

Instructions

The purpose of this step is the selection and planning of instruments--tests, questionnaires, diaries, etc.--that will give you the largest amount of information possible.

a. Make an Outcomes Table with four vertical numbered columns

 In Column 1 list the outcomes common to both Programs X and C that you have chosen to measure. These are the circled objectives on the Objectives Worksheet, pages 76 and 77, plus additions you have made as a result of discussions and reading or based on your own hunches. If you intend to measure outcomes unique to one of the programs, list these as well, but remember that Programs X and C are not competitors regarding these.

Outcomes Table

1 Outcomes	2 Circle C, A, P or O*	3 Instrument chosen	4 To be given to whom?
1.	C A P O		
2.	C A P O		
3.	C A P O		
4.	C A P O		
etc.			
Those unique to X:			
1.	C A P O		
2.	C A P O		
etc.			
Those unique to C:			
1.	C A P O		
2.	C A P O		
etc.			

*Cognitive, Affective, Psychomotor, or Other

 For advice about measuring cognitive or psychomotor objectives, see How To Measure Achievement. If objectives are affective, see How To Measure Attitudes.

 For each objective, list the instrument chosen in Column 3 and the recipients of the instrument in Column 4.

b. Make a four-column Implementation Table

List in Column 1 the materials, activities, and organizational arrangements in Program X and Program C for which you will collect backup data.

Implementation Table

1 Materials, activities, organizational arrangements	2 Instruments chosen	3 To be given at what sites?	4 To be administered to whom?
Of Program X			
1.			
2.			
3.			
4.			
etc.			
Of Program C			
1.			
2.			
etc.			

 Consult How To Measure Program Implementation for suggestions about ways to collect backup data to support your description of program activities.

 Then enter in Column 2 the instruments you have chosen to use. In Column 3 list the sites at which implementation of that feature can be observed or recorded. Finally, list recipients of the instrument in Column 4.

C. <u>Decide how you will measure costs</u>

 Choose which instruments will give
you the information you need, and
enter these instruments into a
three-column <u>Costs Table</u>.

Costs Table

1 Costs	2 Instruments chosen	3 To be given to whom?
1.		
2.		
3.		
4.		
etc.		

Consolidate your concerns into a few instruments

If you want to collect a maximum amount of information per instrument, try the following quick exercise in re-listing. If you are satisfied that your list of instruments is efficient, or if it is very small, skip this step.

In the interest of economy of time and money, and so that your evaluation is not intrusive on the program, try to administer only one instrument of a particular type--questionnaire, interview, test, etc.--to each group of respondents. For example, do not give teachers a questionnaire on costs and a questionnaire on attitudes. Consolidate concerns about outcomes, implementation, and costs into single instruments.

 If your evaluation focuses on many concerns and several types of instruments will be administered, then try filling in a three-column table to organize your thoughts:

1 Instrument chosen	2 To be given to whom?	3 Outcome, activity, or cost (and its number from Step 2)
1.		
2.		
3.		
4.		
etc.		

 To complete the table, go back and look at the outcomes, aspects of program implementation, and costs you listed on the tables you completed in Step 2 of this phase.

Then:

- List in Column 1 each instrument you have chosen to administer.

- In Column 2, note the group to whom it will be given (teachers, School Board, etc.)

- In the third column, list the evaluation concerns--outcomes, implementation characteristics, costs, and their numbers--that the instrument will cover.

When an instrument and a to whom listed in Columns 1 and 2 match a pair that has already been listed, enter only the corresponding concern into Column 3. This will allow you to collect concerns per instrument, producing lists like this:

1 Instrument chosen	2 To be given to whom?	3 Outcome, activity, or cost (and its number from Step 2)
Question-naire	Teachers	Outcome #4 Cost #1 Activity #3

In this case, you will be able to construct a single questionnaire	To be given to teachers	To cover all three concerns

 When you have completed the instrument consolidation exercise, ask yourself:

☐ Can I collect yet more information? _____

Look for instruments that will cover only <u>one</u> evaluation concern--for example:

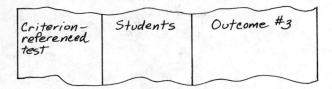

Then ask yourself:

☐ Could I add to the value of using the instrument by measuring a concern listed in Phase A that I did not bring forward to the tables in Step 2, Phase B?

 Go back over the worksheets you completed when you listed major features of the program during Phase A. With a little extra effort, you might add a new concern that can be easily measured. For example, if you have chosen to use "observation" to measure the implementation of a behavior modification system in the classroom, it might be useful for you to add <u>another activity</u> that your observer could keep track of-- say, topics of instruction in math, or length of time spent on reading--to the list of concerns. This will allow you to take maximum advantage of the instruments you administer.

If you can think of <u>no</u> outcomes, activities, or costs to be added to instruments now measuring only one, then consider one final question:

☐ Is that <u>one</u> single concern worth the effort of devoting one whole instrument--with all the time and effort involved in construction, administration, and scoring--to it?

If the concern is of high priority and you--or your audience--<u>must</u> know about it, then the answer is YES. Use the instrument. If the answer is NO, then eliminate the instrument and try to measure that concern in some other way.

Step 4

Plan the construction and purchase of instruments

Instructions

Once you have a list of the instruments you will administer, use this step to help you manage their acquisition and plan their use.

 If you suspect that you have listed more instruments that you can realistically make or purchase and administer within the time and cost limits of your evaluation, then do this: Complete Step 8 in this phase to get a more realistic perspective on how much the evaluation will cost. If you still think your measurement plans are too ambitious, select a few instruments that measure the outcomes, activities, or costs that you feel are most important, and obtain these instruments first. If time and funds are available, you can acquire the others later.

 Find out, as well, whether members of the program's staff are willing to help with collecting data. Explain to program directors and staff members that their cooperation will allow you to collect richer and more credible information about the program—to present, in the end, a clearer and more fair picture of what has been accomplished.

Ask them in particular:

☐ Can records kept during the program as a matter of course be collected or copied to provide information for the evaluation?_____

_____

☐ Can record-keeping systems be established and maintained to give the needed evaluation information?_____

☐ Will teachers and staff be able to share achievement information with the evaluator or help with its collection? Are you willing to administer instruments to samples of students?

_____

☐ Will one or more staff members be willing to assist with collecting information, constructing, or scoring instruments, or overseeing proper implementation of the evaluation design?

_____

_____

 How To Measure Program Implementation, pages 79 to 88, describes a method for establishing a record-keeping system to keep track of program activities during its evaluation.

 Now is the time to delegate responsibilities. You will be able to relieve yourself of some of the burden for conducting this evaluation by finding staff members or volunteers from local schools and colleges. These people can order and construct instruments, see to their administration, and set up the evaluation design described in Step 6 of Phase B and Step 2 of Phase C. Choose a staff member, a department head, teacher, secretary, or assistant, and describe the instrument or design set-up you need.

 Lend your assistants copies of a How To Measure book that describes construction or purchase of the instruments you need. Or give them How To Design a Program Evaluation. Agree together on deadlines for construction or acquisition as well as administration of instruments. Step 1 of Phase C will help you to set realistic deadlines.

 Build a schedule. Use a table like the one on the following page to record your decisions about construction, purchase, and delegation of responsibilities regarding instruments. The relevant How To books give form letters and memos for ordering tests from publishers.

Instrument Management Table

1 Instrument chosen	2 Made in-house or purchased?	3 Person responsible for construction	4 Date instrument to be received or completed

 Various books in the Program Evaluation Kit contain advice on constructing instruments. The relevant How To books guide you in construction or revision of:

Checklists	How To Measure Program Implementation and How To Measure Attitudes
Interviews	How To Measure Attitudes and How To Measure Program Implementation
Achievement tests	How To Measure Achievement
Observation schedules	How To Measure Program Implementation and How To Measure Attitudes
Questionnaires for different age groups	How To Measure Attitudes and How To Measure Program Implementation
Records	How To Measure Program Implementation
Attitude rating scales	How To Measure Attitudes
Sociometric instruments	How To Measure Attitudes

Step 5

Plan the data analysis you will perform with the results from each instrument

Instructions

As soon as you have decided what instruments you will use and have roughed out the contents of each, plan how you will analyze the data that each will produce. Considering data analysis _early_ in the evaluation will prevent you from wasting time collecting information you will not use--or worse yet, collecting the right information, but in a form too unwieldy to be used.

 Each of the measurement books in the _Program Evaluation Kit_ makes suggestions for summarizing, analyzing, and displaying data.

In	See pages
How To Measure Attitudes	74-75, 159-177
How To Measure Achievement	125-145
How To Measure Program Implementation	64-77

How To Design a Program Evaluation contains tables, graphs and analyses associated with each of the evaluation designs you might choose. Try to collect information in the form that can be most easily presented and discussed.

How To Calculate Statistics describes come of the more straightforward analyses you might perform. If you want more complex statistics, consult a data analyst. Carefully examine the match between the analyses you plan to use and the measures you are planning before you become too deeply enmeshed in constructing instruments.

 If at all possible, plan mechanical data processing and computer analysis. These are discussed in the Kit's measurement books. For a more detailed description of computer data analysis, see _How To Calculate Statistics_, Chapter 5.

Choose evaluation designs

Instructions

An evaluation design is a <u>plan</u> of <u>who</u> will receive each measurement instrument you decide to administer and <u>when</u>. The quality of the design directly affects the usefulness of each evaluation instrument's results.

 Read pages 16 to 19 of this <u>Handbook</u> These present an argument for using designs in evaluation. If you have not yet read <u>How To Design a Program Evaluation</u>, look at Chapters 1 and 2 now. This book discusses six designs in detail and gives directions for implementing each one.

 Choose a design to guide administration of each instrument. Read <u>How To Design a Program Evaluation</u>, pages 48 to 51, and the following discussion about designs. Then decide which ones you can implement.

Because it is usually inconvenient--and unnecessary--to use a separate design per instrument, choose one or two to underpin the whole evaluation. Designs 1, 2, 3, and 5 are the most useful for gathering interpretable information. One of these should underlie data-gathering for at least some of the measures--tests, questionnaires, interviews, etc.--you intend to measure.

In addition to the timing and placement of measures, the <u>evaluation design</u> prescribes who gets exposed to the <u>program</u>. In order to implement Designs 1 and 2, you will have to have some influence over whether students or other participants can be randomly assigned to programs. In order to implement Designs 3 or 5, you will have to find a non-randomized comparison group.

In short, for Designs 1, 2, 3, and 5, you will usually have to be in the position of planning the evaluation <u>before</u> the program gets underway. Since not every evaluator finds himself in this position, Designs 4 and 6 are adequate where nothing else is possible.

Design 1: True Control Group

 This design is ideal for choosing between Program X and another program since it measures exactly how Program X measures up against an alternative. The other program--Program C--might be a pre-existing program, or it might be a competitor or control program. Whatever the other program is, in order to implement this design, both Program X and Program C should be running at the same time.

Procedure

a. Identify all students or classes who can get either Program X or Program C.

b. Pretest this group.

c. <u>Randomly</u> divide the students or classes into two groups, and give one group Program X and the other group Program C.

d. Make sure that:

- There is as little difference as possible in what happens to the two groups apart from the Program X/Program C difference--that is, avoid <u>confounds</u>.

- Program X and Program C stay distinct, not sharing or joining forces--that is, they avoid <u>contamination</u>.

e. Posttest both groups simultaneously.

Chapter 5, a <u>Step-by-Step Guide for Conducting a Small Experiment</u>, is an example of a true control group evaluation. If you choose either Design 1 or Design 2 for any of your measures, and if you can meet the preconditions listed in Step 1 on page 108 of Chapter 5, then use that Step-by-Step Guide. Its prescription about how to evaluate is more detailed than this chapter's.

Design 2: True Control Group
With Posttest Only

This design is identical to Design 1 except the pretest--step b--is omitted. This design is useful when the experience of the pretest might itself interfere with program effects. This might be the case, for example, if a questionnaire were administered at the beginning of a program intended to change attitudes, thereby flagging for participants the program's intended effects. A pretest might also be unavailable or inconvenient to give.

Randomization in this design assures equivalence of the groups receiving the two programs.

Design 3: Non-Equivalent Control Group

This is a good design for choosing between Program X and some other program, Program C, which will also be in operation during the period of the evaluation. As in Designs 1 and 2, Program C might be a control group or a competitor with Program X.

This design enables you to compare the results of Programs X and C on two groups which are similar even though they were not randomly assigned and are therefore not equivalent as in Designs 1 and 2.

Procedure

a. Find a similar group of students, at the same grade level, who will be given Program C in the same time period that a group will be given Program X. How To Design a Program Evaluation gives suggestions for doing this.

b. Pretest both groups of students, and collect information on both groups concerning characteristics which might affect their reactions to Programs X or C.

c. Investigate differences in what happens to the group getting Program X and the group getting Program C if these differences are likely to affect results.

d. Posttest both groups.

Design 4: Single Group Time Series

A series of measurements made during and/or after Program X gives a good picture of the impact of Program X on whatever is measured. This design requires scores collected from the same group on several occasions before Program X and on several occasions during and after Program X. The scores should be based on the same measuring instrument.

Design 5: Time Series With
Non-Equivalent Control Group

This design involves making measurements exactly as in Design 4. But here, two groups of students are measured regularly--the group receiving Program X, and the other, a non-equivalent control group, not randomly assigned--like the one used in Design 3.

Design 6: Before-and-After Design
Allowing Informal Comparisons Only

Design 1 and Design 2 are experimental designs because both Program X and a comparable or control program, C, are implemented to see which produces better results: a little experiment is run. If only Program X can be measured, then the only way to interpret the results of the measurements will be by comparing pretest and posttest results, or by making informal comparisons based on published data, school records, or predetermined standards. You might make one or all of the following comparisons:

☐ Comparison of pretest and posttest results for Program X

☐ Comparison of Program X results with results from a national sample of students, the norm group for a standardized test. A national sample of students is used as a comparison group whenever you use results expressed as percentiles, grade equivalents, or stanines.

☐ Comparison of Program X results with results described in curriculum materials

☐ Comparison of Program X results with results obtained by last year's students at the same grade level

☐ Comparison of Program X results with prespecified criteria; for example, "80% of students will achieve 75% of grade two math objectives." Such criteria may have been set up by teachers, the community, or the district; or they may have been specified in a program plan.

Step 7

Choose a sampling strategy for administering instruments

Instructions

If either Program X or Program C is a large one with many participants at diverse sites, you will not be able to measure all the members of each group prescribed by your evaluation design or to look at implementation at every site. You will have to sample people to test, question, or observe, and possibly sites on which to focus as well.

 Sampling plans for making data collection more manageable are discussed at several places in the Kit. See How To Deal With Goals and Objectives, pages 56 to 62; How To Design a Program Evaluation, pages 157 to 161; and How To Measure Program Implementation, pages 60 to 65.

Choice of which sites to measure depends on the questions you want to answer. If the program varies considerably from site to site, you should include in your selection representatives of each version of the program. This will be particularly crucial if you are exploring the relative effects of different planned or natural variations in the program. If the program is intended to be uniform across sites, choose sites based on other criteria such as the length of time the program has been in operation at the site, the amount of experience of teachers, the characteristics of neighborhoods involved, or the amount of funds allotted to the program.

 If you have been unable to obtain a comparison group, consider the possibility of using different versions of the program as Program X and Program C--or perhaps the same program at qualitatively different sites.

 Record your decisions:

☐ Program X sites will be sampled

Number of Program X sites to be sampled_____

On what basis?_____

_____

☐ Program C sites will be sampled

Number of Program C sites to be sampled_____

On what basis?_____

_____

☐ Programs X and C will represent different versions of the same program. These versions are:

- Program X_____

  Number of sites_____

- Program C_____

  Number of sites_____

☐ Programs X and C will represent the same program implemented at different sites:

- Program X sites have this characteristic

  _____

  Number of sites_____

- Program C sites have this characteristic

  _____

  Number of sites_____

 In order to produce a representative description of the program, find out the optimal or most typical times to test students, question people, and observe program implementation at each site. Record these, and keep them in mind when scheduling the dates of data collection in Step 1, Phase C.

Estimate the cost of the evaluation

Instructions

If your activities will be financed from the program budget, you will have to determine early the financial boundaries of the service you provide. The cost of an evaluation is difficult to predict accurately. This is unfortunate, since what you will be able to promise the staff and planners will be determined by what you feel you can afford to do.

Estimate costs by getting the easy ones out of the way first. Find out costs per unit for each of these "fixed" expenses:

☐ Postage and shipping (bulk rate, _____ parcel post, etc.)

☐ Photocopying and printing _____

☐ Travel and transportation _____

☐ Long-distance phone calls _____

☐ Test and instrument purchase _____

☐ Consultants _____

☐ Mechanical test or questionnaire _____ scoring

☐ Data processing _____

These fixed costs will come "off the top" each time you sketch out the budget accompanying an alternative method for evaluating the program.

The most difficult cost to estimate is the most important one: the price of person-hours required for your services and those of the staff you assemble for the evaluation. If you are inexperienced, try to emulate other people. Ask how other evaluators estimate costs and then do likewise.

Develop a rule-of-thumb that computes the cost of each type of evaluation staff member per unit time period, such as "It costs $4,500 for one senior evaluator, working full time, per month." This figure should summarize all expenses of the evaluation, excluding only overhead costs unique to a particular study--such as travel and data analysis.

The staff cost per unit figure should include:

Salary of a staff member for that time unit

+ Benefits

+ Office and equipment   ⎤
rental   ⎟ This equals the total
                          ⎟ routine expenses of
+ Secretarial services   ⎟ running your office
                          → for the time unit in
+ Photo copying and   ⎟ question, divided by
duplicating   ⎟ the number of full-
                          ⎟ time evaluators
+ Telephone   ⎟ working there
                          ⎟
+ Utilities   ⎦

Compute such a figure for each salary classification--Ph.D's, Masters' level staff, data gatherers, etc. Since the cost of each of these staff positions will differ, you can plan variously priced evaluations by juggling amounts of time to be spent on the evaluation by staff members in different salary brackets.

The tasks you promise to perform will in turn determine and be determined by the amount of time you can allot to the evaluation from different staff levels. An evaluation will cost more if it requires the attention of the most skilled and highly priced evaluators on your staff. This will be the case with studies requiring extensive planning and complicated analyses. Evaluations that use a simple design and routine data collection by graduate students or teachers will be correspondingly less costly.

 To estimate the cost of your evaluation, try these steps:

a. Compute a cost-of-staff-per-unit-time figure for each job position occupied by someone who will work on the evaluation.

Depending on the amount of backup staff support entered into the equation, this figure could be as high as twice the gross salary earned by a person in that position.

b. Calculate a first estimate of which staff members' services will be required for the evaluation, and how long each will need to work.

c. <u>Estimate the evaluation's total cost</u>.

Refer to the proposed time span of the evaluation. Be sure to include fixed costs unique to the evaluation --travel, printing, long-distance phone calls, etc.--and your indirect or overhead costs, if any. Discuss this figure with the funding source, or compare it with the amount you know to be already earmarked for the evaluation.

d. <u>Trim</u>.

Rather than visiting an entire population of program sites, for instance, visit a small sample of them, perhaps a third; send observers with checklists to a slightly larger sample, and perhaps send questionnaires to the whole group of sites to corroborate the findings from the visits and observations. See if one or more of the following strategies will reduce your requirment for expensive personnel time, or trim some of the fixed costs.

☐ Sampling

☐ Employing junior staff members for some of the design, data gathering, and report writing tasks

☐ Finding volunteer help, perhaps by persuading the staff that you can supply richer and more varied information or reach more sites if you have their cooperation

☐ Purchasing measures rather than designing your own

☐ Cutting planning time by building the evaluation on procedures that you, or people whose expertise you can easily tap, have used before

☐ Consolidating instruments and the times of their administration

☐ Planning to look at different sites with different degrees of thoroughness, concentrating your efforts on those factors of greater importance

☐ Using pencil-and-paper instruments that can be machine read and scored, where possible

☐ Relying more heavily on information that will be collected by others, such as state-administered tests, and records that are part of the program

---

Instructions

At this point, the program evaluation has been
thoroughly planned and is getting underway. The
purpose of Phase C is to help you through the
process of data collection. By this time, what
remains is to see that everything proceeds as
expected.

The steps in Phase C can be summarized as follows:

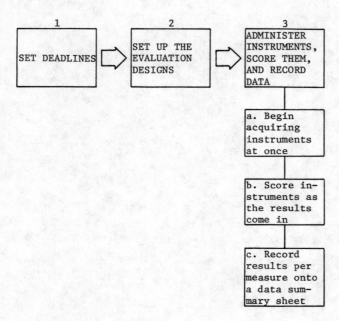

Instructions

 The following table should help you keep track of instrument development, administration, scoring, and data recording.

Instrument Use Table

1	2	3		4	5
		Adminis-tration deadlines			
Instru-ment	Completion/receipt deadline	pre	post	Scoring deadline	Recording deadline

 Each of the How To Measure books in the Program Evaluation Kit contains suggestions for administering the instruments you are using as well as detailed directions for recording, scoring, and summarizing their results.

 Fill in deadlines for each phase of the instrument's use:

- Completed construction or receipt from a publisher
- Administration
- Scoring
- Recording of scores

A good rule-of-thumb to follow regarding deadlines is this:

- Start with the deadline for your evaluation report, and subtract three weeks. This is your latest possible deadline for recording all scores --column 5. Make the deadline earlier if you think you will need more than three weeks to

analyze data, draw charts and graphs, and write the final report. This, of course, will depend on the number of instruments you are using and the formality of your analysis and report.

- Set the scoring deadline in column 4 according to the amount of help you will have. If a dele-gated person can record scores from the instru-ments fairly quickly, then set scoring a few days prior to recording.

The following should help you to schedule times for test administration, column 3:

- The posttest should be given as near as possible to the end of the program to allow the program to have a maximum amount of time to work its effect. Do not, however, be alarmed if it turns out that you will need to give the posttest at a time when only 85% or so of the program time has elapsed--in early May, perhaps, for a program that runs the course of a school year. In most cases, the program will have a had a chance to show its effect by then. Besides, it has been argued that testing in the last few weeks, or days, of a program, when people are unwinding for its termination, may actually reflect its effect less well than testing earlier. In other words, it is possible that program effects will peak at the point of about 85% to 95% elapsed time.

- Plan to posttest well before the scoring deadline, particularly if instruments must be sent away for scoring. For difficult-to-score tests, you might have to allow several weeks. Be mindful that when you have chosen to rely on state-wide tests, you are at their mercy for receiving scores.

- The time of administration of the pretest should, in most cases, coincide with the beginning of the program. An exception to this is the situ-ation in which the pretest is used as a basis for assigning students to programs via blocking or stratified sampling. If the pretest is to be used as a basis for assignment of students, then it should be given well before the program begins.

<u>How To Design a Program Evaluation</u>, pages 34 to 43, contains additional details about when, how and why, to schedule pretests and posttests.

- With regard to the <u>Completion/Receipt Deadline</u>, column 2, make sure that you schedule receipt of the instrument at least a week-to-10 days before the administration deadline. This should allow for delays without seriously jeopardizing the rest of your schedule. Remember that <u>constructing</u> a test or questionnaire generally requires several drafts and tryouts.

Set up the evaluation designs

Instructions

In Phase B you selected instruments with which to carry out measurements and you chose an evaluation design to determine when--and to whom--they would be administered. The purpose of this step is to help you ensure that the design is carried out.

 Issues of design and random assignment are treated in depth in How To Design a Program Evaluation. In this book you will also find step-by-step directions for setting up any of the six designs you have chosen to use.

The three checklists which follow are intended to help you keep track of the implementation of the design you have chosen. Set up the checklist that is relevant to your particular design. Use it to keep track of important information and to check the completion of activities essential to the design.

Checklist for a Control Group Design With Pretest--Designs 1, 2, and 3

1. Name the person responsible for setting up the design_____

If the design uses a true control group:

2. Will there be blocking? ☐ yes   ☐ no

   (See How To Design a Program Evaluation, pages 149 and 150.)

3. If yes, based upon what?
   ☐ ability   ☐ sex
   ☐ achievement   ☐ other_____

4. Has randomization been completed?
   ☐ yes   ☐ no   Date_____

If the design uses a non-equivalent control group:

5. Name this group_____

---

6. List the major differences between the program and comparison groups--for example, sex, SES, ability, time of day of class, geographical location, age:
   _____
   _____
   _____

7. Has contact been made to secure the cooperation of the comparison group? ☐ yes
   Date_____

8. Agreement received from (Ms./Mr.)_____

9. Agreement was in the form of (letter/memo/ personal conversation/etc.)_____

10. Confirmatory letter or memo sent? ☐ yes
   Date_____

11. Is there a list of students receiving the comparison program? ☐ yes   ☐ no
   Where is it?_____

In either case:

12. Name of pretest_____

13. Pretest completed? ☐ yes   Date_____

14. Teachers (or other program implementors) warned:
   ☐ To avoid confounds? Memo sent or meeting held (date)_____
   ☐ To avoid contamination? Memo sent or meeting held (date)_____

   (See How To Design a Program Evaluation, page 60.)

15. List of possible confounds and contaminations
   _____
   _____
   _____

16. Check made that both programs will span the same time period? ☐   Date_____

17. Posttest given? ☐   Date_____

<u>Checklist for a Time Series Design</u>
<u>With Optional Non-Equivalent Control Group</u>
<u>--Designs 4 and 5</u>

1. Name of person responsible for setting up and maintaining design_____

2. Names of instruments to be administered and readministered_____

3. Equivalent form of instruments to be:
   ☐ Made in-house?   ☐ Purchased?

4. Number of repeated measurements to be made per instrument_____

5. Dates of planned measurements:
   ☐ 1st_____   ☐ 5th_____
   ☐ 2nd_____   ☐ 6th_____
   ☐ 3rd_____   Additional:
   ☐ 4th_____   ☐ _____

If the design uses a control group:

6. Name of control group_____

7. List of major differences between the program group and the control group--for example, sex, SES, ability, geographical location, age
_____
_____

8. Contact made to secure cooperation of comparison group? ☐ Date_____

9. Agreement received from (Ms./Mr.)_____

10. Confirmatory letter or memo sent? ☐
    Date_____

11. List of possible contaminations
_____
_____
_____

<u>Checklist for Pre-Post Design</u>
<u>With Informal Comparisons--Design 6</u>

1. Name of person responsible for setting up design_____

2. Comparison to be made between obtained <u>post-test</u> results and <u>pretest</u> results? ☐
   • Name(s) of instrument(s) to be used
_____
_____

• Equivalent forms of instruments to be:
   ☐ made   ☐ purchased

• List of students receiving Form A on pretest and Form B on posttest_____
_____
_____

• List of students receiving Form B on pretest and Form A on posttest_____
_____
_____

• Dates of planned measurements:
   Pretest_____   Completed? ☐
   Posttest_____   Completed? ☐

3. Comparison to be made via standardized tests? ☐
   • Name of standardized test(s)_____
_____
   • Test given? ☐ Date_____
   • Scoring and ranking of program students completed? ☐ Date_____

4. Comparison to be made between obtained results and results described in curriculum materials? ☐
   • Name of curriculum materials_____
_____
   • Unit test results collected and filed? ☐
   • Unit test results from program graphed or otherwise compared to norm group? ☐

5. Comparison to be made between results from a previous year and the results of the program group? ☐
   • Which results from last year will be used-- for example, grades, district-wide tests?
_____
   • Last year's results tabulated and graphed? ☐
   • List made of possible differences between this and last year's (or last time's) group that might differentially affect results? ☐
_____
_____
   • Program X's results collected? ☐
   • Program X's results scored and graphed, or otherwise compared, with last year's? ☐

6. Comparison to be made between obtained results and prespecified criteria about attainment of program objectives? ☐

- Whose criteria are these--for example, teachers, district, curriculum developers?
  _____

- State the criteria to be met_____
  _____
  _____

- Objectives-based test results collected and filed? ☐

- Objectives-based test results graphed, or otherwise compared, with criterion? ☐

CHECK ✓ ☐ If you have chosen to administer instruments at only a sample of program sites or to a sample of respondents, then use the following table to keep track of the proper implementation of your sampling plan.

Sampling Plan Checklist

1. The sample will ensure adequate representation to different types of:
   ☐ Sites--what kinds?_____
   ☐ Time periods--which ones?_____
   ☐ Program units--which ones?_____
   ☐ Program roles--which ones?_____
   ☐ Student or staff characteristics--name them
   _____

   ☐ Other_____

2. The sampling plan comprises a matrix or cube with _____ cells (see How To Measure Program Implementation, pages 60 to 65)

3. How many cases will be sampled from each cell? _____ (see How To Design a Program Evaluation, pages 157-161, for suggestions about selecting random samples)

4. Cases selected? ☐

5. For each time selected:
   - Have instruments been administered? ☐
   Comments_____
   - What deviations from the sampling plan have occurred?_____
   _____

Step 3

Administer instruments, score them, and record data

a. <u>Once you have decided which instruments to use, begin acquiring them at once</u>. Have no illusions--ordering and constructing instruments will take a long time, possibly months.

If you intend to <u>buy</u> instruments, use the form letters in the various <u>How To</u> books for ordering them. Check the list of test publishers in the <u>How To</u> books for sources of published tests.

If you plan to construct your own instruments, <u>write a memo</u> to those in charge of producing them, leaving no doubt about who is responsible and deadlines for their completion.

Instruments made in-house must be tried out, debugged, and evaluated for technical quality. To aid the process, the Kit's measurement books discuss reliability and validity as they apply to the three primary measurement concerns treated in the books. See <u>Achievement</u>, Chapter 5, <u>Attitudes</u>, Chapter 11, and <u>Implementation</u>, Chapter 7. A little run-through with a few students or aides might mean the difference between a mediocre instrument and a really excellent one.

Keep tabs on instrument orders. If you have not received them within two weeks of the deadline, prod the publisher or your in-house developer.

<u>Once each instrument is completed or received, plan how it will be scored and recorded</u>:

b. <u>Score instruments as the results come in</u>

If the instrument has a <u>selected</u> response format-- for instance, multiple-choice, true-false, Likert-scale--make sure you have a scoring key or template.

If it has an <u>open-ended</u> format, make sure you have a set of correctness criteria for scoring, or a way of categorizing and coding questionnaire or interview responses.

See <u>How To Measure Program Implementation</u>, pages 71-73 and <u>How To Measure Attitudes</u>, pages 106 and 107, and 170 and 171. These sections contain information about scoring or coding open-response items, essays, and reports. If the test is to be scored elsewhere by a state or district office or by an agency with whom you have a contract for testing and scoring, and you are to receive a print-out of the results, <u>decide whether you wish to score sections of it for your own purposes</u>. In some cases, achievement of objectives can be measured via partial scoring of a standardized test.

See <u>How To Deal With Goals and Objectives</u>, pages 43 to 46, and <u>How To Measure Achievement</u>, pages 36 to 39 for a description of a technique for doing this.

c. <u>Record results per measure onto a data summary sheet</u>

Once you know what the scores from your instruments will look like, decide whether you want results for each examinee, mean results for each class, or percentage results for each item. Then, when each instrument has been administered, score the instruments as soon as possible.

Once scoring is completed, consult the appropriate <u>How To</u> books for suggestions about formatting and filling out data summary sheets. See <u>Attitudes</u>, pages 159 to 166; <u>Implementation</u>, pages 67 to 71; and <u>Achievement</u>, pages 117 to 120.

Construct separate data summary sheets for Program X people and the comparison group so that it is impossible to get them confused. Then delegate the scoring and recording tasks.

Phase D
Analyze Data

Instructions

The data of your evaluation are the <u>recorded</u> <u>scores</u> from the instruments you administered. By the time you have finished Phase C, all the data are <u>there</u>. The purpose of Phase D is to help you to conduct the analyses you choose.

The steps in Phase D are as follows:

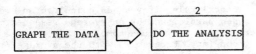

Instructions

Your data analysis should begin with a graph--even a rough one--to allow you to look for trends and regularities in your results. At times the graph, if it shows a glaringly clear trend, will be all you need to support your report conclusions.

 The How To books concerned with measuring attitudes, achievement, and program implementation describe graphing methods for scores obtained from every type of instrument described in the Kit. Graphs are also discussed in Chapter 4 of How To Present an Evaluation Report, and Chapter 1 of How To Calculate Statistics.

You should graph results even when all you intend to report is average scores per group--for instance, "The average reading score for Program X was 10 raw score points higher than for Program C." In these cases, graph the average scores per group according to characteristics such as grade level, sex, SES, or ability. Graphing will help you uncover much information that you did not know you had.

So, for each instrument administered, plan to produce at least one graph.

 You do not have to do statistical tests to produce a good report. However, doing them will make your conclusions stronger.

 How To Calculate Statistics describes statistical tests that can be performed by anyone who can multiply and divide. Don't decide against performing statistics because you think it will be too complex.

Whether or not you can perform statistical tests depends on the design of the evaluation and the measurements you made. If you have used one of the group comparison designs--Designs 1, 2, 3, and 5-- you can perform statistical tests that show the significance of the difference between the scores of the two groups, that is, whether the difference could have occurred by chance. If you are using Design 6, you can do a statistical test only under these circumstances:

- If you are comparing performance of the program group on a standardized test with that of the test's norm group and the standard deviation of that group's scores is available, or

- If your reference group is last year's or last time's group, or you are comparing pretest and posttest results for the same group.

 How To Design a Program Evaluation discusses these situations in greater detail.

As a general rule, if you can calculate an average score per participant or an average response per question, and if you can compare this average for one group (say, Program X) with the average from another group (Program C), then you can do a statistical test.

Step 2

Do the analysis

Instructions

How To Calculate Statistics details procedures for summarizing scores through indicators of central tendency, such as the mean, and indicators of score variability, such as the standard deviation; performing tests for statistical significance; and calculating measures of relationship such as correlations. For more complex analyses, consult a data analyst.

If you are using mechanical scoring or data processing, then set up the appropriate data files and proceed with the analysis.

A table like the one below will help you keep track of data analysis:

Data Analysis Table

1 Instrument	2 Will results be graphed?	3 Graph format chosen--refer to page # in How To book	4 Statistical analysis to be done

List instruments you have scored in column 1. Then, consult the How To book most closely related to each instrument, design, or analysis, and follow its suggestions concerning graphing. Mark your decision about whether or not to graph and indicate the graph format to be used--you might even sketch this--in column 3.

Finally, in column 4, list the statistical analyses --tests for significance, correlations, etc.--to be performed.

When each graph and statistical test is completed, examine it carefully and write a one-or-two sentence description that summarizes your conclusions from reading the graph and noting the results of the analysis.

Save the graphs and summary sentences that seem to you to give the clearest picture of the program's impact. These can be used as a basis for the Results section of your report.

_____

_____

_____

_____

_____

_____

_____

_____

_____

_____

Phase E
Prepare the Report

Instructions

If you have fairly faithfully followed this Step-
by-Step Guide in designing and carrying out your
evaluation, then by now you are well prepared for
presenting the final report. The logic and
sequence of this guide is the same as that to be
followed in a final report. All that remains now
is for you to put what has been recorded on the
worksheets suggested in this chapter into a
coherent form for your audience.

There are three steps in Phase E:

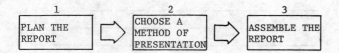

1 PLAN THE REPORT → 2 CHOOSE A METHOD OF PRESENTATION → 3 ASSEMBLE THE REPORT

Step 1

Plan the report

Instructions

How To Present an Evaluation Report gives section-by-section directions for preparing formal and informal reports for many different audiences. Read Chapter 1 and look over the outline in Chapter 2 to help you decide which of the topics apply to your report. If you will need to describe program implementation, look at the report outline in

Chapter 2 of How To Measure Program Implementation. Then write a quick general outline of what you plan to discuss.

Step 2

Choose a method of presentation

Instructions

Decide whether your report to each audience will be oral or written, formal or informal.

Chapter 3 of How To Present an Evaluation Report lists a set of pointers to help you organize what you intend to say and to decide how best to say it.

Instructions

 A worksheet like the one below will help you to record your decisions about reporting and to keep track of the progress of your report.

Final Report Preparation Worksheet

1. List the audiences to receive each report, date reports are due, and type of report to be given to each audience. Some reports may be suitable for more than one audience.

Audience	Date report due
_____	_____
_____	_____
_____	_____
_____	_____
_____	_____

2. How many different reports will you have to prepare?
_____

3. For each different report you submit, complete this section:

Report #1   Audience(s)_____

Checklist for Preparing Evaluation Report:

- Report will be: ☐ formal   ☐ informal
  ☐ oral   ☐ written

- Deadline for finished draft_____
  Completed? ☐

- Deadline for finished audio-visuals, if any
  _____
  Completed? ☐

- Deadline for finished tables and graphs
  _____
  Completed? ☐

- Names of proofreaders of final draft, audio-visuals, or tables

  _____
  Contacted and agreement made? ☐

  _____
  Contacted and agreement made? ☐

  _____
  Contacted and agreement made? ☐

- Date agreed upon as deadline for getting drafts to proofreaders. These are absolute deadlines for completing drafts:
  _____   Draft sent? ☐
  _____   Draft sent? ☐
  _____   Draft sent? ☐

- Dates drafts must be received in order to revise in time for final report deadlines:
  _____   Proofread draft received? ☐
  _____   Proofread draft received? ☐
  _____   Proofread draft received? ☐

This is the end of the Step-by-Step Guide for Conducting a Summative Evaluation. By now evaluation is a familiar topic to you and, hopefully, a growing interest. This guide is designed to be used again and again. Perhaps you will want to use it in the future, each time trying a more elaborate design and more sophisticated measures. Evaluation is a new field. Be assured that people evaluating programs--yourself included-- are breaking new ground.

Chapter 5

Step-by-Step Guide For Conducting a Small Experiment

The self-contained guide which comprises this chapter will be useful if you need a quick but powerful pilot test—or a whole evaluation—of *a definable short-term program or program component*. The guide provides start-to-finish instructions and an appendix containing a sample evaluation report. This step-by-step guide is particularly appropriate for evaluators who wish to assess the effectiveness of *specific materials and/or activities* aimed toward accomplishing a *few specific objectives*.

If a major purpose of the program you are evaluating is to produce achievement results, this guide outlines *an ideal way to find out how good these results are: conduct an experiment.* For a period of days, weeks, or months, give students the program or program component you wish to evaluate while an equivalent group, the *control* group, does not receive it. Then at the end of the period, test both groups. This step-by-step guide shows you how to conduct such an evaluation.

Whenever possible, the step-by-step guide uses checklists and worksheets to help you keep track of what you have decided and found out. Actually, the worksheets might be better called "guidesheets," since you will have to copy many of them onto your own paper rather than use the one in the book. Space simply does not permit the book to provide places to list large quantities of data.

As you use the guide, you will come upon references marked by the symbol ◢. These direct you to read sections of various *How To* books contained in the *Program Evaluation Kit*. At these junctures in the evaluation, it will be necessary for you to review a concept or follow a procedure outlined in one of the Kit's seven resource books:

- *How To Deal With Goals and Objectives*
- *How To Design a Program Evaluation*
- *How To Measure Program Implementation*
- *How To Measure Attitudes*
- *How To Measure Achievement*
- *How To Calculate Statistics*
- *How To Present an Evaluation Report*

Should You Be Using This Step-By-Step Guide?

The appropriateness of this guide depends on whether or not you will be able to set up certain *preconditions* to make the evaluation possible. Check each of the preconditions listed in Step 1. If you can arrange to meet *all* of them, then you can use the evaluation strategy presented in this guide. As you assess the preconditions, you will be taking the first step in planning the evaluation. This step-by-step guide lists 13 steps in all. A flow chart showing relationships among these steps appears in Figure 5. You may wish to check off the steps as they are accomplished.

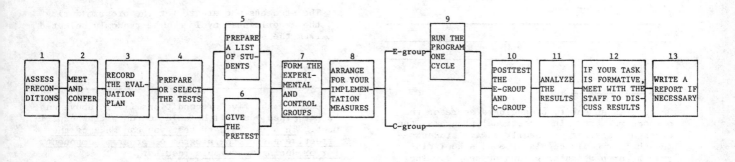

Figure 5. The steps for accomplishing a small experiment, listed in this guide

Instructions

CHECK ✓ ☐ <u>Put a check in each box if the pre-condition can be met</u>. For the first three preconditions, there are some decisions to be recorded on the lines provided. Record these decisions in pencil since you may change them later. This step-by-step guide will be useful to you only if you can meet <u>all five preconditions</u>.

☐ PRECONDITION 1. <u>An outcome measure will be available</u>.

A test can be made or selected to measure what students are supposed to learn from the program. Write down what the outcome measure(s) will probably be:

_____

_____

_____

☐ PRECONDITION 2. <u>A sample of cases* can be defined</u>.

You can list at least 12, say, students for whom this program would be suitable and for whom, therefore, the outcome measure is an appropriate test of what they learned in the program. Write down the criteria that will be used to select students for the sample:

_____

_____

_____

_____

*A <u>case</u> is an entity producing a score on the outcome measure. In educational programs, the cases of interest are nearly always students--though they could be classrooms, school districts, or particular groups of people. The word <u>student</u> is used throughout the guide. If the cases in your situation are different, just substitute your own term.

☐ PRECONDITION 3. <u>A time period--a cycle--can be identified</u>.

You can identify a time period which is of a duration appropriate to teach the skills the outcome measure taps. Call this period of time one <u>cycle</u> of the program. Write down what length of time one cycle of the program will probably last:

_____

_____

_____

☐ PRECONDITION 4. <u>An experimental group and a control group can be set up</u>.

For one cycle at least, one group of students in the sample will get the program and another will not. If the program can run through several cycles, this does not mean that some students will <u>never</u> get the program, just that they must wait their turn. In this way, no students are left out--a concern which sometimes makes people unwilling to run an experiment.

☐ PRECONDITION 5. <u>Students who are to get the program can be randomly selected</u>.

The students who are to get the program during the experimental cycle will be randomly selected from the sample.

If each of the five preconditions listed above can be met, then you will be able to run a true experiment. <u>This is the best test you can make of the effectiveness of the program or program component for producing measurable results</u>.

Meet and Confer

Instructions

This step helps you work out a number of practical details that must be settled before you can complete your plans for the pilot test or evaluation.

 You will need to meet and confer with the people whose cooperation you need and, possibly, with members of other evaluation audiences. You will need to reach agreement with them about:

☐ How the study should be run

☐ How to identify students for the program

☐ What program the control group should receive

☐ The appropriate outcome measure

☐ Whether to use additional measures

☐ What procedures will be used to measure implementation

☐ To whom results will be reported--and how

How Should the Study Be Run?

 In particular, are students to receive the program in addition to regular instruction or instead of regular instruction? If the program is to be used in addition to regular instruction, students will have to be pulled out for the program sometime other than the regular instruction period. A means of scheduling will need to be agreed upon.

How Should Students Be Identified for the Sample?

 It might be that the sample will simply be all the students in a certain class or classes. On the other hand, perhaps the program is intended only for students who have a certain need or meet some criterion. In this case, you will need to agree upon clear selection criteria. If the program is remedial, selection might be based on low scores on a pretest, or you might use teacher nominations. Test scores for selection

are preferred if the outcome measure is to be a test. The problem with basing selection on an existing set of test scores is that they might be incomplete; scores might be missing for some students. You could use the outcome measure as a selection pretest.

 How To Design a Program Evaluation, pages 35 and 36, discusses selection tests. See also How To Measure Achievement, pages 124 and 125.

How many students will you need? The more the better, but certainly you should avoid ending up with fewer than six pairs of students, a total of 12. If during the program cycle, one student in a pair is absent too often or fails to take the posttest, the pair will have to be dropped from the analysis. The longer the cycle, the more likely it is that you will lose pairs in this way. Bearing this in mind, be sure to select a large enough sample. If it looks as if the sample will be too small--perhaps because the program has limited materials--you should abandon an experimental test or run the experiment several times with different groups each time and then combine results to perform a single analysis.

What Program Should the Control Group Receive?

 If one group of students will get the program and a control group will not, the question arises about exactly what should happen to the control group. Should the control group receive no instruction in the subject matter to be taught by the program? For example, if program students leave the classroom to work on computer assisted instruction in fractions, should the control students receive instruction in fractions as well, or should they spend their time on something else altogether?

It is best to set up the experiment to match the way in which the program will be used in the future. If the program will be used as an adjunct to regular instruction, then set up the experiment so that the experimental group gets the program in addition to the regular program. If the program, on the other hand, is a replacement for regular instruction, then the control group will get only regular instruction and the experimental group will get only the program. If you are interested in assessing the effectiveness of two separate programs, either of which might replace the regular one, then give one to the experimental group and one to the control.

 How To Design a Program Evaluation discusses what should happen to control groups on pages 29 to 32.

What Outcome Measure--Posttest--Is Reasonable for Detecting the Effect of One Cycle of the Experiment?

 The posttest must meet the requirements of a good test. It should therefore be:

• Adequately long to have good reliability

• Representative of all the relevant objectives of the program, to demonstrate content validity

• Clearly understandable to the students

 A good posttest is essential. Whether you plan to purchase it or construct it yourself, refer to How To Measure Achievement.

Do You Need Other Measures in Addition to the Outcome Measure?

 Will the posttest provide a sufficient basis on which to judge the program? If the posttest contains many items which reflect specific details of the program--special vocabulary, for instance, or math problems that use a particular format--then a high posttest score may not represent much growth in general skills. In such a case, you might want to use an additional posttest for measuring achievement that contains more general items.

Since an immediate posttest will measure the initial impact of a program, you may wish to measure retention by administering another test some time later. You may, in addition, need to measure other program outcomes such as the attitudes of students, parents, or teachers.

 See How To Measure Achievement and How To Measure Attitudes

What Procedures Will Be Used for Measuring Program Implementation?

 As the program runs through a cycle, a record should be kept of which students actually participated in the program and which students--perhaps because of absences--did not. You must also keep careful track of what the experiences of program and control students looked like.

 See How To Measure Program Implementation.

Which Groups of People Will Be Informed About the Results?

CHECK ☑ ☐   Check relevant audiences:

☐ Teachers of students involved

☐ The program's planners and curriculum designers

☐ Other teachers

☐ Principals

☐ District personnel

☐ Parents of students involved

☐ Other parents

☐ Board members

☐ Community groups

☐ State groups

☐ The media

☐ Teachers' organizations

Do meetings need to be held with any of these groups, either to give information or to hear their concerns, or for both reasons?

☐ Yes   ☐ No

If yes, hold such meetings.

 You and the others involved have now finished deciding how to do the evaluation. Once these decisions are firm, go back to Step 1 and change the preconditions entries you made there if necessary.

Record the Evaluation Plan

Instructions

Construct and complete a worksheet like the one
below, summarizing the decisions made during
Step 2. Contents of the worksheet can be used
later as a first draft of parts of the evaluation
report.

If two programs or components are being compared,
and each is equally likely to be adopted, then you
will have to carefully describe both.

PROGRAM DESCRIPTION WORKSHEET

This worksheet is written in the past tense so
that when you have completed it you will have a
first draft of two sections of your report: those
 that describe the program and the
evaluation. For more specific help
with deciding what to say, consult
How To Present an Evaluation Report.

Background Information About the Program

A. Origin of the Program

_____
_____
_____

B. Goals of the Program

_____
_____
_____

C. Characteristics of the Program--materials,
    activities, and administrative arrangements

_____
_____
_____
_____

_____
_____
_____
_____
_____
_____
_____
_____

D. Students Involved in the Program

_____
_____
_____
_____
_____
_____

E. Faculty and Others Involved in the Program

_____
_____
_____
_____

Purpose of the Evaluation Study

A. Purposes of the Evaluation

_____
_____
_____
_____
_____
_____
_____

B. Evaluation Design

A pretest-posttest true experiment was used to
assess the impact of the program on student
achievement. The target sample consisted of
all who (fill in the selection criteria here)

_____

_____

Experimental and control groups were formed by
random selection from pairs of students
matched on the basis of the pretest.

C. Outcome Measures

_____

_____

_____

_____

_____

_____

D. Implementation Measures

_____

_____

_____

_____

_____

_____

_____

Once you have completed the Worksheet, you have
prepared descriptions of the program and of the
evaluation. These descriptions will serve as your
first draft of the evaluation report.

Prepare or Select the Tests

Instructions

The Pretest

Use one of three kinds of pretests:

• A test to identify the sample of students eligible for the program--this is a <u>selection test</u>

• A <u>test of ability</u> given because you believe ability will affect results, and you therefore want the average abilities of the experimental and control groups to be roughly equal

• A <u>pretest which is the same as the posttest</u>, or its equivalent, so that you can be sure that the posttest shows a gain in knowledge that was not there before

In most cases, the pretest should be the posttest or the outcome measure itself. If this will be possible in your situation, then produce a thorough test which will be used as both pretest and posttest.

Preparing the Pretest Yourself

 <u>How To Measure Achievement</u>, Chapter 3, lists resources, item banks, and guides to help you construct a test yourself. <u>How To Measure Attitudes</u> gives step-by-step directions for constructing attitude measures of all sorts.

Once the test has been written, try it out with a small sample of students to ensure that it is understandable and that it yields an appropriate pattern of scores for a pretest--not too many high scores so that there is room at the top for students to show growth. The tryout students should <u>not</u> be students who will be assigned to either the experimental or control groups. You will need at least five students for the tryout. They should be as similar as possible to the students who are to receive the program. You might need to borrow students from another class or school.

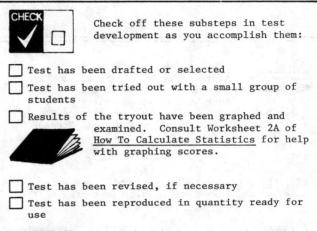 Check off these substeps in test development as you accomplish them:

☐ Test has been drafted or selected

☐ Test has been tried out with a small group of students

☐ Results of the tryout have been graphed and examined. Consult Worksheet 2A of <u>How To Calculate Statistics</u> for help with graphing scores.

☐ Test has been revised, if necessary

☐ Test has been reproduced in quantity ready for use

 If you intend to use the pretest you have purchased or written for <u>selection</u> of students, then you will, of course, have to administer the test <u>before</u> you decide which students are eligible. In this case, complete Step 6 before Step 5.

If the pretest will be administered to program and control groups <u>after</u> the groups have been formed, then go on next to Step 5.

Prepare a List of Students

Instructions

 List all students for whom one cycle of the program will be appropriate. In order to construct this list, you must have a set of <u>criteria for selection</u>. These should have been established in Step 1 and recorded on the worksheet in Step 3.

Write the names of the students who meet the selection criteria down the left hand side of the paper. Call this a <u>sample list</u>.

If you are using the selection test as a pretest as well, <u>list students in order by score</u>, from highest to lowest, and record each student's score next to his or her name.

Your sample list might look like this:

```
        SAMPLE LIST

Adams, Jane
Bellows, John
Cartwright, Jack
Dayton, Maurice
Dearborn, Fred

Eaton, Susie
James, Alice
Markham, Mark
Payne, Tom
Pine, Judy

Taylor, Harvey
Vine, Grace
Washington, Roger
Williams, Greg
```

Give the Pretest

Instructions

It is best to give the pretest at one sitting to all students concerned. Be sure no copies of the test are lost. <u>All</u> tests handed out must be returned at the end of the testing period. For obvious reasons, this is <u>critical</u> if the test will be used again as a posttest.

Tests are more likely to get lost when they use a separate answer sheet which is also collected separately. If your test uses a separate answer sheet, then have students place answer sheets inside the test booklet, and collect the two together.

Form the Experimental and Control Groups

Instructions

a. Record pretest scores on the sample list if you have not already done so.

b. Graph the pretest scores

Refer to Worksheet 2A of How To Calculate Statistics for help with this step.

Are the scores appropriate for a pretest? That is, are scores relatively spread out with few students achieving the maximum? If yes, continue.

If the test was too easy, prepare and give another test with more difficult items. The program's instructional plans might need revision too if a test well-matched to the program's objectives was too easy for the target students.

c. Rank order the students according to pretest scores

If it is not already arranged according to student scores, rewrite the sample list starting with the student with the highest score and working down to the lowest.

d. Form "matched" pairs

Draw a line under the top two students, the next two, and so on.

Bellows	38
Eaton	36
Adams	35
Dayton	35
James	35
Payne	32
Dearborn	31
Vine	30

e. From each pair, randomly assign one student to the experimental group and the other student to the control group

To accomplish the random assignment, toss a coin. Call the experimental group or E-group "heads" and the control or C-group "tails." If a toss for the first person in the first pair gives you heads, assign this person to the E-group by putting an E by his name. His match, the other person in the pair, is then assigned to the C-group. If you get tails, the first person in the pair goes to the C-group and the other to the E-group.

Repeat the coin toss for each pair, assigning the first person according to the coin toss and his match to the other group. If there is an odd number of students, just randomly assign the odd student to one or the other group, but do not count him in the analysis later.

f. Prepare a Data Sheet

Have a list of the E-group and C-group students typed on a Data Sheet. This sheet should place the E-group at the left-hand side with a column for the posttest scores, then the C-group and the score column at the right. Always keep matched pairs on the same row. Columns 5, 6, and 7 will contain calculations to be performed later.

DATA SHEET

1 E-group	2 Post-test	3 C-group	4 Post-test	5 d	6 $(d-\bar{d})$	7 $(d-\bar{d})^2$

Instructions

Ensure that the program has been implemented as
planned. This means ensuring that the students
who are supposed to get the program--the E-group
--do get it, and the others--the C-group--do not.

To accomplish this, try the following:

* <u>Work closely with teachers</u> to assure that the
  program groups receive the program at the
  appropriate times. Arrange a plan for carefully monitoring student absences from the
  program.

* <u>Set up a record-keeping system</u> to verify implementation of the program. For example, students
  could sign a log book as they arrive for the
  program, or perhaps they could turn in their
  work after each session. In addition, if possible, plan to have observers record whether the
  program in action looks the way it has been
  described.

 Refer back to the worksheet in
Step 3 (<u>Implementation Measures</u>)
to review your decisions on how to
measure program implementation.

 Check <u>How To Measure Program Imple-
mentation</u> for suggestions about
collecting information to describe
the program.

Step 9

Run the Program One Cycle

Instructions

Let the program run as naturally as possible, but check that accurate records are kept of the students' exposure to the program.

 Be careful. If teachers or the evaluator pay extra attention to experimental group students, this alone could cause superior learning from them. So be as unobtrusive as possible.

Step 10

Posttest the E-group and C-group

Instructions

Give the posttest to the experimental and control groups at one sitting, if possible, so that testing conditions are the same for all students. If one sitting is not possible, test half the experimental group along with half the control group at one sitting and the others at a second sitting.

Of course, some of your outcome measures might not be tests as such. Interviews, observations, or whatever, should also be obtained from the experimental and control groups under conditions that are as similar as possible.

If necessary, schedule make-up tests for students absent from the posttest.

Instructions

a. Score the Posttests

If the test you have constructed yourself contains closed response items--for example, multiple choice, true-false--then you can delegate someone to score the tests for you. How To Measure Achievement, pages 117 to 120, contains suggestions for scoring and recording results from your own tests.

b. Check the Data Set and Prune as Necessary

Use the Sample List to complete this procedure:

Check for absences from the program. If some students in either the experimental or control group missed a lot of school during the program's experimental cycle, they they should be dropped from the sample. You and your audience will have to agree about how many absences will require dropping the student from the analysis. One day's absence in a cycle of one week would probably be significant since it represents 20% of program time. A week's absence in a six month program, on the other hand, could probably be ignored.

If you decide that students in the experimental group should be dropped from the analysis if their absences exceeded, say, six days during the program, then control group students absent six or more days should also be dropped. This keeps the two groups comparable in composition. If the control group received a program representing a critical competitor to the program in question, then control group absences should be noted as well and the Sample List pruned accordingly.

 From attendance records, determine the number of days each student was absent during the program cycle. Record this information in appropriately labeled columns added to the Sample List. Drop all students whose absences

exceeded a tolerable amount for inclusion in the experiment. For every student dropped, the corresponding control group match will have to be dropped also. Drop as well any student for whom there is no posttest score. Drop his match also.

c. Summarize Attrition

Summarize results from pruning of the data in the table below. The number dropped from each group is called its "mortality" or "attrition."

TABLE OF ATTRITION DATA
Number of Students Remaining in the Study
After Attrition for Various Reasons

	Experimental Group	Control Group
Number assigned on basis of pretest		
Number dropped because of excessive absence from school during program		
Number dropped from E-group because of failure to receive program although in school		
Number dropped because of lack of posttest score		
Number dropped because match was dropped		
Number retained for analysis		

d. Record Posttest Scores on the Data Sheet for Students Who Have Remained in the Analysis

Instructions

e. Test To See if the Difference in Posttest Scores Is Significant

Were you to record just any two sets of posttest scores, it is likely that one of the groups would have higher scores than the other just by chance. What you now need to ask is whether the difference you will almost inevitably find between the E- and C-group posttest scores is so slight that it could have occurred by chance alone.

 The logic underlying tests of statistical significance is described in How To Calculate Statistics. In fact, pages 71-76 of that book discuss the t-test for matched groups, to be used here, in detail.

To decide whether one or the other has scored significantly higher in this situation, you will use a correlated t-test--correlated because of the matched pairs used to form the two groups. Using your data, you will calculate a statistic, t. You will then compare this obtained value of t with values in a table. If your obtained value is bigger than the one in the table, the tabled t-value, then you can reject the idea that the results were just due to chance. You will have a statistically significant result. Below are the steps for this procedure.

Steps for Calculating and Testing t

Calculate t

This is the formula for t:

$$t = \frac{(\overline{d})\,(\sqrt{n})}{s_d}$$

In order to calculate it, you need to first compute the three quantities in the formula:

$\overline{d}$ = average difference score

$\sqrt{n}$ = the square root of the number of matched pairs

s_d = the standard deviation of the difference scores

Use the data sheet from Step 7 to help you calculate quantities for the t equation.

DATA SHEET

1 E-group	2 Post-test	3 C-group	4 Post-test	5 d	6 $(d-\overline{d})$	7 $(d-\overline{d})^2$

Page 126 shows a data sheet that has been computed.

To compute $\overline{d}$. First find the difference between the scores on the posttests for each pair of students. The difference, d, for a pair is the quantity:

$$\left[\begin{array}{c}\text{posttest score}\\\text{of the E-group}\\\text{student}\end{array}\right] - \left[\begin{array}{c}\text{posttest score of}\\\text{the matched C-}\\\text{group student}\end{array}\right]$$

Note that whenever a C-group student has scored higher than an E-group student, the difference is a negative number. Record these differences in Column 5 of the Data Sheet.

Then add up the entries in Column 5 and divide that sum by the number of pairs being used in the analysis, n. This gives you the average difference between the E-group and C-group. Call it $\overline{d}$, read "d bar."

$$\boxed{} = \overline{d}$$

To compute s_d. Fill in the quantities for Columns 6 and 7. For Column 6, subtract $\overline{d}$ from each value in Column 5, and record the result. For Column 7, square each number in Column 6 and divide their sum by n-1, the number that is one less than the number of pairs. Take the square root of your last answer and record this below as s_d.

$$\boxed{} = s_d$$

To compute $\sqrt{n}$. Take the square root of the number of matched pairs--not the number of students--which you are using in the analysis. This $\sqrt{n}$. Enter it here:

$$\boxed{} = \sqrt{n}$$

Instructions

<u>To compute t</u>. Now enter these values in the
formula for t below:

$$t = \frac{(\overline{d})\ (\sqrt{n})}{s_d} =$$

Multiply the top line. Then divide the result
by s_d to get your t-value. Enter it here:

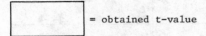 = obtained t-value

Find the Tabled t-value

Using the table below, go down the left-hand
column until you reach the number which is equal
to the <u>number of matched pairs</u> you were analyzing.
Be careful to use the number of <u>pairs</u>, not the
number of students.

Table of t-Values for Correlated Means

Number of matched pairs	Tabled t-value for a 10% probability (one-tailed test)
6	1.48
7	1.44
8	1.41
9	1.40
10	1.38
11	1.37
12	1.36
13	1.36
14	1.35
15	1.34
16	1.34
17	1.33
18	1.33
19	1.32
20	1.32
21	1.32
22	1.32
23	1.32
24	1.32
25	1.31
26	1.31
.	.
40	1.30
.	.
120	1.29

The t-value in the left-hand column that corres-
ponds to the number of <u>matched pairs</u> is your
tabled t-value. Enter it here:

= tabled t-value

Interpret the t-test

If the obtained t-value is <u>greater</u> than the tabled
t-value, then you have shown that the program significantly improved the scores of students who got
it. If your obtained t-value is less, then there
is more than a 10% chance that the results were
just due to chance. Such results are not usually
considered statistically significant. The program
has not been shown to make a statistically significant difference on this test.

The test of statistical significance which you
have used here allows a 10% chance that you will
claim a significant difference when the results
were in fact only due to chance. If you want to
make a firmer claim, use the Table of t-values in
Appendix B. This table allows only a 5% chance of
making such an error.

A good procedure in any case is to repeat the program another cycle and again perform this evalua-
tion-by-experiment--only this time, use the 5%
table to test the results. If your results are
again significant, you will have very strong
grounds for asserting that the program makes a
statistically significant difference in results
on the outcome measure.

Construct a Graph of Scores

If results <u>were</u> statistically significant, display
them graphically. Figures A and B present two
appropriate ways to do this. Figure A requires
fewer calculations.

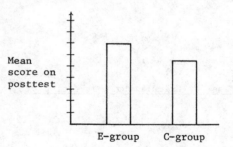

<u>Figure A</u>. Posttest means of
groups formed from matched pairs

Instructions

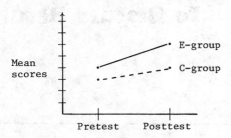

Figure B. Pretest and posttest mean
scores of experimental and control
groups

You may wish to take a closer look at the results
than just examining averages or single tests of
significance. Taking a close look will further
help you interpret results. In particular, if
the results were not statistically significant,
you may want to look for general trends.

One good way to take a closer look at results is
to compute the gain score--posttest minus pretest
--for each student. Using gain scores, you can
plot two bar graphs, one showing gain scores in
the experimental group and the other showing gain
scores in the control group. If some students'
scores were quite extreme, look into these cases.
Perhaps there was some special condition, such as
illness or coaching, which explains extreme scores.
If so, these students' scores should be dropped
and the t-test for differences in posttest scores
computed again.

If Your Task Is Formative, Meet With the Staff To Discuss Results

---

Instructions

The agenda for this meeting should have an outline something like the following:

Introduction

Review the contents of the worksheet in Step 3, pages 111 and 112.

Presentation of Results

Display and discuss the attrition table which describes student absences from the experimental and control groups. Display Figures A and B and discuss them. Report the results of the test of significance.

Discussion of the Results

If the difference was significant as hypothesized --the E-group did better than the C-group--you will need to answer these questions:

• Was the result <u>educationally</u> significant? That is, was the difference between the E-group and the C-group large enough to be of educational value?

• Were the results heavily influenced by a few dramatic gains or losses?

• Were the gains worth the effort involved in implementing the program?

If the results were non-significant, you will need to consider:

• Do you think this was due to <u>too short a time span</u> to give the program a fair chance to show its effects, or was the program a poor one?

• Were there special problems which could be remedied?

• Was the result <u>nearly</u> significant?

• Should the program be tried again, perhaps with improvements?

Recommendations

On the basis of the results, what recommendations can be made? Should the program be expanded? Should another evaluation be conducted to get firmer results--perhaps using more students? Can the program be improved? Could the evaluation be improved? Collect and discuss recommendations.

Write a Report if Necessary

Instructions

 Use as resources the book <u>How To Present an Evaluation Report</u> and the worksheet in Step 3 of this guide. The worksheet, you will remember, contains an early draft of the sections of the report that describe the program and the evaluation.

You have reached the end of the Step-by-Step Guide for Conducting a Small Experiment. The guide, however, has two appendices:

• Appendix A contains an example of an evaluation report prepared using this guide.

• Appendix B contains the table of values for performing a t-test of statistical significance at the 5% level.

Appendix A

Example of an Evaluation Report

This example--which is fictitious and should not be interpreted as evidence for or against any particular counseling method--illustrates how an experiment can form the nucleus of an evaluation. Notice that information from the experiment does not form the sole content of the report. The evaluator has to consider many contextual, program-specific pieces of information, such as the exact nature of the program, the possible bias that might be introduced into the data by the information available to the respondents, etc. There is no substitute for thoughtfulness and common sense in interpreting an evaluation.

EVALUATION REPORT

Program	The Preventive Counseling Program
Program location	Naughton High School
Evaluator	J. P. Simon, Principal Naughton High School
Report submitted to	J. Ross, Director of Evaluation Mimieux School District
Period covered by report	January 6, 19xx-February 16, 19xx
Date report submitted	March 31, 19xx

Section I. Summary

A new counseling technique based on "reality therapy" and the motto that "prevention is better than cure" was developed by the Mimieux School District and consultants.

Naughton High School evaluated this Preventive Counseling Program by making it available to one group of students, but not to a matched control group.

Results of teacher ratings subsequent to the Preventive Counseling Program and a count of the number of referrals to the office, both pointed to the success of the PC program at least on this short-term basis.

This evaluation report details these findings and presents a series of recommendations for further evaluation of this promising program.

Section II. Background Information Concerning The Preventive Counseling Program

A. Origin of the Program

Several counselors had received special training, at district expense, in a style of counseling related to "reality therapy." This counseling was designed to be used with students whom teachers felt were "heading for trouble" in school or not adjusting well to school life. By an intensive course of counseling, it was hoped to prevent future problems, hence the title the Preventive Counseling Program. The district office asked Naughton High School to assess the effectiveness of this kind of counseling. A counselor trained in the technique was made available to the school on a trial basis for four hours a day over a two week period.

B. Goal of the Program

The goal of the Preventive Counseling Program (PC) was to promote successful adjustment to school among students whom teachers referred to the office.

C. Characteristics of the Program

In the PC program, a student who is referred by a teacher receives an initial 20 minutes of counseling. Follow-up counseling sessions are given to the student each day for the next two weeks.

This program differs from methods used previously to handle referrals to the office. Previously, teachers were not encouraged to refer students to the office. When a student was referred for some particular reason, he generally received one counseling session and perhaps no follow-up at all, unless the teacher referred the student again. This kind of counseling was the responsibility of the usual counseling staff or, in exceptional cases, the vice-principal.

The PC program:

1. Uses counselors who are specially trained in "reality therapy" counseling

2. Requests referrals before an incident necessitates referral

3. Gives the student two weeks of counseling

D. Students Involved in the Program

The counseling is appropriate for students of all grade levels. Any student referred by a teacher is eligible for counseling. During the trial period for this evaluation, however, only some referred students could receive the PC program.

E. Faculty and Others Involved in the Program

As far as possible, the counselor and teachers communicated directly regarding students in need of counseling. A clerk handled scheduling of counseling sessions, managing this in addition to his other duties.

Section III. Description of
the Evaluation Study

A. Purposes of the Evaluation

The District Office wanted Naughton High School to evaluate the effectiveness of the new style of counseling. The study in this school was to be one of several studies conducted to assist the District in deciding whether or not to have other counselors receive reality therapy training and conduct preventive counseling.

Several School Board members had emphasized that they were interested in seeing firm evidence, not opinions.

B. Evaluation Design

In view of the costly decisions to be made and the desire of the Board members for "hard data," the evaluation was designed to measure the results of the PC program as objectively and accurately as possible. To accomplish this, it was deemed necessary to use a true control group. Teachers were asked to name students in their classes who were in need of counseling. For each student named, the teacher provided a rating of the student's adjustment to school on a 5-point scale

from "extremely poor" to "needs a little improvement." This was called the adjustment rating.

Students referred by three or more teachers formed the sample used in the evaluation. An average adjustment rating was calculated for each of the sample students by adding together all ratings for a student and dividing by the number of ratings for that student. These students were then grouped by grade and sex. Matched pairs were formed by matching students (within a group) with close to the same average ratings.

From these matched pairs, students were randomly assigned to receive the new counseling (the Experimental or E-group) or to be the Control group or C-group. Should students from the control group be referred for counseling because of some incident, for example, then the regular counselors were requested to counsel as they had in the past. The E-group students received the two weeks of counseling which is characteristic of the PC program.

At the end of the two-week cycle, all referrals to the office were again dealt with by regular counselors or the vice-principal. Over the next four weeks, records of referrals to the office were kept. If the number of referrals to the office was significantly fewer for the students who had received the PC program (i.e., the E-group students), then the program would be inferred to have been successful.

This measure is reasonably objective and the random assignment of students from matched pairs ensured the initial similarity of the two groups, thus making it possible to conclude that any difference in subsequent rates was due to the PC program.

C. Outcome Measures

As mentioned above, the effect of the program was measured by counting, from office records, how many times each control group student and how many times each experimental group student was referred to the office in the four weeks after the intervention program ended.

An unavoidable problem was that teachers were sometimes aware of which students had been receiving the regular counseling, since students were called to the office regularly for two weeks from their classes. Teachers might have been influenced by this fact. In order to reduce the possible impact of this situation on teacher referral behavior, the fact that the evaluation was being conducted was not made known until after the data collection period was over (four weeks after the Preventive Counseling program ended).

A second measure of outcomes was also collected: teachers were asked at the end of the data collection period to re-rate all students previously identified as needing counseling, giving a "student adjustment rating" on the same 5-point scale which had been used in the beginning of the program.

D. Implementation Measures

The counselor's records provided the documentation for the program. Essentially, these records were used to verify that only E-group students had received the Preventive Counseling program and to record any absences which might require that the student not be counted in the evaluation results.

Section IV. Results

A. Results of Implementation Measures

Eighteen pairs of students were formed from teachers' referrals. The 18 students in the E-group had a perfect attendance record during the Preventive Counseling program and did not miss any counseling sessions. However, two students in the control group were absent for a week. These students and their matched pairs were not counted in the analysis thus leaving a total of 16 matched pairs.

B. Results of Outcome Measures

Table 1 shows the number of referrals to the office from the experimental and control groups during each of the four weeks following the end of the PC program.

TABLE 1
Number of Referrals to the Office

	# of referrals to office				
	Week 1	Week 2	Week 3	Week 4	Total
E-group (had received PC)	1	1	1	2	5
C-group (had not received PC)	3	2	3	2	10

There were twice as many referrals (10 as opposed to 5) in the control group as in the experimental group. Closer analysis revealed that four of the referrals in the E-group were produced by one student who was referred to the office each week. Checking the number of students referred at least once (as opposed to the total number of referrals), it was found that there were two for the experimental and six for the control group.

The second set of averaged school adjustment ratings collected from teachers is recorded in Figure 1, and the calculations for a test of the significance of the results are presented in the same figure. The t-test for correlated means was used to examine the hypothesis that the E-group's average adjustment ratings would be higher, after the program, than those of the C-group. The hypothesis could be accepted with only a 10% chance that the obtained difference was simply the result of chance sampling fluctuations. The obtained t-value was 2.06, and the tabled t-value (.10 level) was 1.34.

DATA SHEET

E-group		C-group				
	Final average adjustment		Final average adjustment			
Student	rating	Student	rating	d	$(d-\bar{d})$	$(d-\bar{d})^2$
AK	3	WK	1	2	1.38	1.90
GF	2	LJ	2	0	- .62	0.38
ST	4	CF	1	3	2.38	5.66
CT	4	LM	3	1	0.38	0.14
JB	3	MH	3	0	-0.62	0.38
SK	3	FH	4	-1	-1.62	2.62
UL	5	DH	5	0	-0.62	0.38
MQ	5	RR	4	1	0.38	0.14
JJ	3	XT	1	2	1.38	1.90
WV	2	KN	2	0	- .62	0.38
AC	4	JR	3	1	0.38	0.14
CK	3	OF	4	-1	-1.62	2.62
CR	2	PD	1	1	0.38	0.14
RA	5	NW	5	0	-0.62	0.38
PG	3	JM	4	-1	-1.62	2.62
FW	4	RL	2	2	1.38	1.90
n = 16			10			21.68

$$\bar{d} = \frac{13-3}{16} \qquad s_d = \sqrt{\frac{21.68}{15}}$$

$$= \frac{10}{16} \qquad = \sqrt{1.44}$$

$\sqrt{n} = 4$ \qquad $\bar{d} = 0.62$ \qquad $s_d = 1.20$

$$t = \frac{(\bar{d})\,(\sqrt{n})}{s_d}$$

$$t = \frac{(0.62)\,(4)}{1.20} = \frac{2.48}{1.20} = \boxed{2.06}$$

Figure 1

C. Informal Results

Several teachers commented informally about the counseling that their problem students were receiving. One said the counseling seemed to be less "touchy feely" and more "getting down to specifics," and she noted an increase in task orientation in a counselee in her room beginning at about the second week of special counseling. She felt, however, that the counseling should have continued longer. Other teachers did not seem to have ascertained the style of counseling being used, but commented that counseling seemed to be having less transitory effect than usual.

A parent of one of the counselees in the PC program called the principal to praise the consistent help his child was getting from the special counselor. "I think this might turn him around," the parent said.

Negative comments came from one teacher who complained that one of her students always seemed to miss some important activity by being summoned to the counseling sessions. Another teacher, however, commented that it was a relief to have the counselee gone for a little while each day.

Section V. Discussion of Results

The use of a true experimental design enables the results reported above to be interpreted with some confidence. Initially, the E-group and C-group were composed of very similar students because of the procedure of matching and random assignment. The E-group received preventive counseling whereas the C-group did not. In the four weeks following the program, all students were in their regular programs and during this time, students from the C-group received twice as many referrals to the office as students from the E-group.

In interpreting this measure, it should be remembered that referral to the office is a quite objective behavioral measure of the effect of the program. It appears that the Preventive Counseling program substantially reduced the number of referrals to the office over this four week period. Whether this difference will continue is not known at this time.

The average post-counseling ratings which teachers assigned to students in the E-group and in the C-group showed a significant difference in favor of the E-group. A problem in interpreting this result is that the teachers were aware of which students had been in the counseling program and this might have affected their ratings. However, 52 teachers were involved in these ratings, some rating only one student and others rating more. That the result was in the same direction as the behavioral measure lends both measures additional credibility.

Section VI. Cost-Benefit Considerations

The program appears to have an initially beneficial effect. However, it also is a fairly expensive program. There are two main expenses involved: the cost of training counselors in reality therapy and the cost of providing the counseling time in the school. There was no way in this evaluation of determining if the training had an important influence on the program's effectiveness. It could have been that other program characteristics--its preventive approach or the continuous daily counseling--were the influential characteristics. Training in reality therapy could possibly be dispensed with thus saving some of the expense. However, since training can presumably have lasting effects on a counselor, its cost over the long-run is not great and comes nowhere near approaching the cost of the provision of counseling time each day.

It is understood that a cost-benefit analysis will be conducted by the District office using results from several schools. One question needing consideration is whether the Preventive Counseling program will in fact save personnel time in the long run by catching minor problems before they develop into major problems. To answer such a question requires the collection of data over a longer time period than the few weeks employed in this evaluation. If the program helps students to overcome classroom problems, then its benefits--although perhaps immeasurable--might be great.

Section VII. Conclusions and Recommendations

A. Conclusions

In this small scale experiment, the Preventive Counseling program appeared to be superior to normal practice. It produced better adjustment to school, as rated by teachers, and resulted in fewer teacher referrals to the office in the four weeks following the end of the two week PC program. It was not possible to determine, from this small study, the extent to which each of the program's main characteristics was important to the success of the overall program.

B. Recommendations Regarding the Program

1. The Preventive Counseling program is promising and should be continued for further evaluation.

2. Preventive Counseling without the reality therapy training might be instituted on a trial basis.

C. Recommendations Regarding Subsequent Evaluation of the Program

1. The kind of evaluation reported here, an evaluation based on a true experiment and fairly objective measures, should be repeated several

times to check the reliability of the effects of counseling as so measured.

2. In several evaluations of the Preventive Counseling program, the outcome data should be collected over a period of several months to assess long-term effects.

3. The School Board and the schools should be provided with a cost analysis of the counseling program which includes a clear indication of (a) the alternative uses to which the money might be put were it not spent on the PC program, and (b) the cost of other means of assisting students referred by teachers.

4. An evaluation should be designed to measure the relative effectiveness of the following four programs:

    • The Preventive Counseling program

    • The Preventive Counseling program run without reality therapy training

    • Reality therapy provided to regular counselors

    • The usual means of handling referrals

Table of t-Values for Correlated Means

Number of matched pairs	Tabled t-value for a 5% probability (one-tailed test)
6	2.01
7	1.94
8	1.89
9	1.86
10	1.83
11	1.81
12	1.80
13	1.78
14	1.77
15	1.76
16	1.75
17	1.75
18	1.74
19	1.73
20	1.73
21	1.72
22	1.72
23	1.72
24	1.71
25	1.71
26	1.71
.	.
40	1.68
.	.
120	1.65

Step-by-Step Guide for Conducting a Small Experiment

Appendix B
Table of t-Values

Master Index to the Program Evaluation Kit

This index lists topics covered throughout the *Program Evaluation Kit*. Entries therefore indicate book *and* page number. The letter **H** stands for *Evaluator's Handbook*; **G** for *How To Deal With Goals and Objectives*; **D** for *How To Design a Program Evaluation*; **I** for *How To Measure Implementation*; **A** for *How To Measure Attitudes*; **Ac** for *Achievement*; **S** for *Statistics*; and **R** for *How To Present an Evaluation Report*.